Lightworker U

Lightworker

Undercover

Your time is NOW

ANYA SOPHIA MANN

ISBN-13: 978-0995559325
ISBN-10: 0995559325

Published by Ruth Hadikin Associates
Contact: info@RuthHadikin.com

Cover design: Anya Sophia Mann
Image credits: All images ©Anya Sophia Mann

Dedication

To all the lightworkers of the world…

you know who you are!

Thank You

Acknowledgements

Words that guided the rest of my life were said in the most perfect moment by my mentor April Prita Manganiello, *"You can't make a blind man see."* From that epic moment everything in my life made sense: past, present, and future relationships with everyone and everything had the gift of a new perspective. Priceless! Eternal appreciation for the role you play in my life.

For every workshop participant over the years, and those in my coaching practice, I am humbled by your willingness to engage so fully in your personal, spiritual and professional development. Your work in lightening up our world, by facing shadow aspects to walk a clearer journey, is what is shifting our world to higher light. You have graced my life with yours. Thank you for your presence.

It is with great respect and honor that I mention my children and marriage: the greatest catalysts to my spiritual growth and personal development on a Soul level. I am proud of who you are, and love who you be. My world is a better place because of you. With so much love and appreciation. You light up my life.

To my beloved grandchildren, you are the brightest lights in my world. Your incarnation is divinely timed and you are Light Masters here to co-create a better world, weaving your light and raising the consciousness of humanity. I am blessed by you.

To every friend whose love, friendship, and support, lit the way in the shadows of my journey to a more refined higher vibrational way of being. I thank you with all of my being in the most heartfelt way. You each made a difference in my life. I see your light. I feel your love. That is why I never lost my way.

Along the way, all the way, I have met, learned from, and been inspired, encouraged and empowered, by many wise teachers from different traditions and dimensional realms. I am grateful for the capacity to receive the teachings in such a way that I can say 'I remember.' That is what we are all here to do, remember who we really are: Light Beings. Thank you for the awakening.

I am grateful for all the scientists and researchers who are coming together in many ways to discover and prove that we are beings of light. We are not dense in our humanity we are light beings whose time is now.

It is with a Soulful depth of appreciation that I acknowledge my publisher and editor extraordinaire Ruth Hadikin, whose brilliance lights up the path that we have journeyed far and wide for over fifteen years. She is Soul Family. No words can describe the depth and height of my heartfelt gratitude. You can only feel it, and I know you do.

Anya Sophia Mann
November 2016
Colorado, USA

Contents

Foreword

We live in unprecedented times. It seems as though the depth of human suffering is on a scale never before seen in humanity, and yet we also have the potential, through our technology to be more connected than ever.

With this book I am deeply honored to be able to publish this timely message, for these difficult and transformational times. It is more important than ever that we wake up and realize who we really are as human beings, and Anya Sophia Mann is uniquely placed to support us in our journey of awakening.

I first met Anya back in 2000, when she was one of the teleclass leaders on a course I was taking. In all my experience, through healthcare and education training, I had never met such an exquisite facilitator of human development.

It seemed to me that no matter what your goal was, she could support you in getting there. I wondered how she was able to work at such a depth and breadth. There seemed to be no limit to her capacity. I thought she must have studied the work of humanistic psychologist Carl Rogers and/or emotional intelligence in great depth.

Later, when I hired her as my coach, she would come to tell me that she had studied none of these things and that it was simply what she called 'clear space'. She not only introduced me to the idea of clear space, but also to many other concepts, including 'you are the ONE in everyONE.'

At the time I found it rather exciting and scary that my every thought, word, and deed, affected everyone else yet, as she reminded me, that is exactly where our power lies. Years later I was studying Buddhist teachings in some depth, and found that I could understand most of the teachings, because they were analogous to the simple principles that Anya had taught me years earlier. I was also fortunate enough to be able to attend some of her workshops in person, where I witnessed and personally experienced the power and depth of this transformative work.

It is precisely because we are connected and that our every intention, thought, word, and action affects everything else, that we have the power to change this world for the better.

This is how I came to recognize the clarity and deep, simple, truth of what Anya teaches. Her words may seem unusual at first, even paradoxical or Zen-like, yet the truth often lies somewhere right in the middle of a paradox. Don't be misled by the simplicity of the ideas she presents. The simplest principles are often the most profound. One of the greatest gifts I ever gave myself was to stay with it, and practice, until I had the personal experience for myself that validated the simple truth that Anya teaches.

Some of you will already know the truth that you are light. For others it may seem like a far-fetched idea. I was one of the latter. I knew when I closed my eyes all I saw was dark. I remember asking, *"when people say they see the light, are they speaking literally or is it just a metaphor?"* I can now say from experience that you are light, and it is possible to literally see your light, and that of others. It is not a metaphor.

If you are feeling your own spiritual calling, and want to make a contribution to our greater world, then Anya's invitation, which I took her up on (and it works), is to begin where it all begins: *with you in your own world.*

It is my sincere wish for humanity that everyone reading this book goes on to practice the points mentioned within, and becomes a brighter light in our world.

May this book brighten your light and guide you on your path.

Ruth Hadikin
Publisher
Author *"Soul Astrology: how your rising sign reveals your soul path and life purpose"*

England, United Kingdom
December 2016

A Note To Lightworkers ...

Dear Reader and Lightworker,

Thank you so much for being here. Your time, attention, and energy, in deciding to read this book matters to me, and to the many people who will benefit by what you read here and then take out into your world. It is your light that lights up and touches the world of so many people around you, from strangers to family. It is time now to recognize your light, even more than you have ever done before. We are in great need of more light right now, so that the shadow aspects currently being acted out on the planet can dissolve in that light.

The Higher Light of Love is healing. You ARE that light. We are a unified field of light. We are unity consciousness. One by one, we illuminate our world. We live in the light of each other's light and we make the biggest difference when we become more conscious of flowing that light. Our light has a calming, neutralizing influence on the anger and fear currently being activated by crushing world events.

You are not alone, ever. Support comes from the seen and unseen realms that are connecting and communicating in a myriad of ways for the highest good of all concerned. There are angels among us that show up in many forms, to guide us in so many ways. Especially when we feel alone in our struggles and need it the most.

Sometimes when you are about to achieve success you might feel something inside hesitating, at those times you may just need a little nudge of further encouragement. A blessing from the light of another's grace can lighten the load you are carrying.

Infinite intelligence and unconditional love can move through any one of us, at any time, for the higher good. Often in the most ordinary moments and with extraordinary results. Many times you too may feel inspired to help someone in need, and become an 'angel' in their life. Can you see yourself as that lightworker at work in your world?

We are meant for each other. Meant to light the way with

our humanity. We are spirits having a human experience. You were born to shine, glow, and sparkle like children at play, however the journey of life can sometimes dim your light. I know that, which is why I have put my heart and soul into sharing this book with you.

*You see I too know what it means
to be a lightworker.*

*I know experientially what it means
to be a lightworker undercover.*

*I know a lightworker
recognizes a lightworker.*

It takes one to know one.

I am one. I see you!

I wrote this book for you. My prayer is that the sparks of light in this book will ignite, awaken, and intentionally stir your purpose here on the planet. I hope you recognize yourself in it's pages. Everything in you already knows the information pulsing off the pages as you read. The purpose of reading is to simply remind you of who you really are as a being of light, carrying vitally important light codes of information that are at your core.

We all need to feel like someone sees us, hears us, and feels us. Knowing that you matter, and are making a difference, is an innate basic fundamental human need. I hope you will naturally resonate to the message in this book and will choose to share its light-filled information. Because when you do, you will actually be grounding and integrating higher light.

The energy you flow into our world is unique and you are a vital piece of a bigger picture that we are all waking up to and living into. Through this book it is my intention to support you in recognizing that for yourself. When you walk through this world consciously, intentionally sharing your smile, your touch, your words, and your actions, the beneficial impact on the hearts and souls of others is beyond measure.

We need each other, in positive ways, so much right now. It is a feeling that feels good, like you feel when you know you matter. I want that for you. Because you do matter. No matter how big or small your contributions you absolutely do matter. Every life you touch sends the message 'you matter' and, in that, YOU matter too.

It is so important now that you take great care of yourself. Treating yourself well keeps your energy field clear, so your light becomes brighter and more refined. There are lots of tips, tools and techniques throughout the book to support you in that endeavor.

You are sacred space and your life will reflect that when you put 'you' first in the sacred act of self-love. Being self-empowered also connects you to the spiritual confidence that is your real personal power, which raises your vibration, increasing your capacity to emanate light.

When you take care of your inner space, your outer space will shine, and sparkle with the light of you. From there you can lend your light to all, so that they too can lean into your light, and rest a while in rejuvenation. Live in the enlivening light of inspiration. Imagine living inspired all day long in the light of the love that is you. You will become contagious, and people will want to bask in your light. In doing that, they also become more of the light of who they really are.

I encourage you to look at yourself and those around you, especially children, in a new light. Imagine what is possible in this world if we all shine our light. YOU are boundless in how you can share the Divine light of Source, as we light each other up in the most unexpected ways.

Look for what effortlessly pulls you forward, draws you up, and invites you into living in the light of YOU. Everything gets better from there. Your internal world, that inner space that you live from, that motivates and inspires you, is the most perfect place to live from as a way of grounding more higher light on the Earth and into our lives as a human family.

**A lightworker is a human being
emanating a unique ray of light
with a capacity to harmonize our world
through their boundless presence.**

We all know that feeling of 'there's something about that person' when we come in contact with someone who is full of love and light - you feel it and see it sparkling in their eyes, their graceful hand gestures, their inspiring words and their compassionate actions. We are always left feeling better and lighter for having met them and been in their presence.

My clear heartfelt intention for you, in writing this book, is to hopefully leave you feeling better, lighter, brighter, heard, felt, seen and understood in the light of seeing yourself in these pages.

All my life, I have been passionate about the light. I live in gratitude, appreciation and acknowledgement every day, for the unique ways you spread the light, through your light. Especially when no one is looking, or sees how you sparkle a situation like the magic of fairy dust!

May the energy field generated by this book, stay with you like a field of grace in full bloom. May light naturally infuse and permeate you, like the scent of roses as someone passes by, and may you continue receiving that light on a cellular level in a myriad of expressions.

Lightworker, I see you. I know you. I feel you. I encourage you. YOU are the difference we all need to inspire and co-create a greater world for all of us.

Lightworker Undercover – your time is NOW!

Warmly, in the light of love,

Anya

Chapter One

Who IS A Lightworker?

"The flower fills the space with perfume...
the candle with light.
They do nothing
yet they change everything
by their mere presence."

- Nisargadatta

Who IS A Lightworker?

Who is a lightworker? YOU, if you are reading this book. I can say, from one lightworker to another that, as a lightworker, you are a human being emanating a unique ray of light with a capacity to harmonize our world through your boundless presence. Your light is a unique ray in the kaleidoscope of light that makes up the body of humanity. You, as a unique ray of light in that body of humanity, are aware and know in the peace of your heart and Soul that the light of love will change our world.

Your Own Universe (Y. O. U.)

Let's take this world of ours, which sounds really big right now, and bring it right down to 'your world.' The world you live in. Y.O.U. is an acronym for Your Own Universe, of which YOU are at the center. Yes, you are the center of Your Own Universe. You are President and CEO of Y.O.U. Now that's a job title! No one can fill that job except YOU. You're hired! You can never be fired. You can only give the job away to someone else, so who would be your boss then?

The Light of Love Will Change The World

When I say 'the light of love will change the world,' it's important to understand that you don't need to go out 'there' to do anything (although you can). Because you ARE the center of your own universe, you are more powerful than you can possibly imagine. One slight shift in your perspective has a ripple effect that can affect your world, which in turn affects the greater world. Just like a pebble dropping in a pond sends waves rippling out. This is the power of you.

My intention is that you recognize yourself in the pages of this book, to raise conscious awareness as to the qualities that a lightworker moves through the world with. Then you can recognize yourself and others more consciously as beings of light, and appreciate how much lightworkers are greatly needed in these shifting times, to reshape and light up our world.

Before reading further I invite you to go to our Facebook page (https://www.facebook.com/GlobalLightworkers) and take the quiz, *"Are You A Lightworker?"* to become familiar with some of the qualities of a lightworker, and possibly recognize yourself. It's not that a lightworker is better than anyone else they just move through the world with a great inner sense of purpose.

You Matter

My heartfelt wish is that you know you matter. I want you to deeply understand your significance, and your vitally important role to all of humanity in these shifting times. You are here for a reason. A unique reason. You just might recognize that for your self as you read this book.

The light that flows through each and every one of us connects and unifies us. Especially the highest frequency of light, which is the light of love that is a unifier. I have worked with the light of love all of my life in many ways, through coaching, consulting and mentoring. People from all walks of life, from CEO's to nurses, entrepreneurs to doctors, and families, parents, and children, have come to recognize themselves as lightworkers undercover, as they realize and value how they light up so many lives in many moments.

Look At Light As Being On A Spectrum

If we look at light as being on a spectrum with a dimmer switch, do you realize that you can be at choice as to where you are on that spectrum in your life today? Twenty percent? Fifty percent? A hundred percent? Once you become aware of the spectrum of light that you are flowing, then you can be at conscious choice as to how lit up or dimmed down you want to be in any moment. All of us range throughout this spectrum every day. As we journey together through this book I'll be showing you how you can consciously choose to navigate the spectrum of light, by using your feelings as your guidance system, so that you can consciously choose to light up situations and flow higher frequencies of light onto the planet.

Light Is About Being

You innately know what the world needs right now. It is for us to be fired up about the light that we really are, and be in our full expression within that spectrum. We'll also talk about how light isn't really about doing at all. Light is about being. Being who you really are. You might say you're being an 'ambassador of light,' being a 'lightworker,' being a 'light master,' or whatever words resonate for you. However the word that's most important is 'being' and light *is* who you 'be.'

It is so important that you recognize this, that I will be emphasizing this point in many different ways throughout this book.

We Are Beings Of Light

We'll also refer to some of the scientific evidence that we are, in fact, beings of light. Science is proving that your DNA emits light like dancing fireflies, and that the cells in your body right now, no matter where you are in the world, are having a conversation with each other and with other people's cells! Whether you're aware of it or not, your cells are lit up in constant connection and communication! We'll talk about what this means for you, in terms of how you can flow your light in the world, and the beneficial impact that has on those around you.

As science is proving that we are beings of light so, of course, it makes sense that we would have a natural capacity to light each other up and reflect each other's light. Wherever you are on the spectrum of consciously flowing light into the world, you can become totally at choice about that. We'll be looking at how you can become even more conscious of it: and show you how to practice turning your light up and dimming it down, wherever you are, so that you too can experience your capacity to flow light at different frequencies, and the subsequent effects of that out in the world.

Know that in your family, at work, in your community, wherever you are, you can beam, be, and emanate light. Whoever comes into that field, whoever comes into that space of you emanating light, is being lit up. Even if it's simply through the exchange of your eyes, your smile, or your touch. For example, when you're driving you might go through the toll and as you pay your fee in the toll booth, you just flash a smile at the person. Bam! You're exchanging light!

You Can Light Up The World

YES! You CAN light up the world! You ARE lighting up the world! And YOU can become more conscious of it. As Mozart is to a symphony, lightworkers are to the kaleidoscope of humanity. When you consciously share your light, when you consciously shine your light, when you consciously emanate your light, you ARE lighting up the world, and unifying humanity with the weaving of that light.

Your Physical Body Is Your Light Vehicle

Just simply by being in the awareness that you are a light of love emanating into this world, you will make a difference as a result of your light. Really recognize that you ARE that light. It's so exciting to realize that you're so much more than your physical body! Your physical body is like your light 'vehicle' that's beaming you into this world, and beaming you out into the world.

So we'll also be looking at who, what, where, when, why, and how to be a lightworker, and what it means to be a lightworker undercover in the world. Millions of undercover lightworkers are busy every day, working in ordinary, everyday jobs, contributing to families and communities. They know they are flowing their unique light into the world. This can be heard in conversations where you hear the language of light enlightening and lighting up heavy, more difficult, conversations through and with lightheartedness.

The highest vibration of light is the frequency of love. Love unifies. Love heals. So when you are in a space of emanating light from your heart, fully aware of what you're doing, as you think about people in a tragedy, or a world event, or an illness of someone in your family, or at work, know that you are emanating the intelligent healing light of love. Not by doing or directing anything, just by simply allowing yourself to be that light.

Light Is Intelligent

In the space of being light you can bring into your consciousness a person or an event and in that space something intelligent happens with the light. Light is intelligent. It knows exactly where to go and what to do. You don't need to do anything, and you're not imposing anything on anyone. Just be aware of your light. Use your light, and in doing that be sure to be in receivership of even more light. Allow more in your life of what causes you to feel good, as way of raising your vibration and receiving Higher Light.

If ever there was a time for us to really show up and shine in the way that is unique to each of us, it is now. The way that I shine my light is just a little bit different than the way in which you shine your light. There is room for all of us. It's like the kaleidoscope of humanity. We each have a little sparkle, a little speckle of that light that we're going to bring through, creating a beautiful, colorful, world of many shades on the spectrum of light. You came as a particle of light and you will leave as an evolved particle of light. Can you imagine the peace, like the joy we feel when we see a rainbow, that will be experienced by the kaleidoscope of humanity, when we all shine and expand into our light?

The Light of You Is A Beacon

The light of you is a beacon, inviting others to come forward, like a moth to a light bulb, to come towards your light in whatever way they feel a resonance with. Some will be attracted to your light, others won't. And that's okay. There's room for all and everyone has their own unique frequency of light that different people will resonate to. You don't need to be concerned about who will resonate with your light, or not, just shine. The light bulb doesn't need to do anything. It doesn't need to go anywhere to 'give' light to anyone. It doesn't worry about which moths will be attracted to it and which ones won't. It is just there shining, emanating it's own light.

I really invite you from this point forward to see yourself as a bright light in this world. That's when you see beauty in the shapes and the shadows of the dimmer side of humanity's light, as light expresses through the gradations of shades and color. Beauty is simply harmony in physical form. We are here to bring beauty to the world by how we see things, which is what brings harmony. I see beauty in you when you emanate the light that's unifying all of us. So shine uniquely in the world and be that light of YOU. Lightworkers, your time is NOW.

We Need Your Light

Let's journey together through the pages of this book where my clear, heartfelt intention is to spark your light in many ways. Inspiring you to be your version of sparkle, shine, and glow as a lightworker on purpose. We need you because some of us who are living with shadows forget who we really are. Light! Those of us who already know we are beings of light also need your light to nurture and nourish our expansion.

Shedding new light on a subject is what gives it a new perspective. Your vibration of light can cause a shadow frequency to lighten up, through your words, contribution, or response, to a person, place or situation. Changing frequency, by raising your dimmer switch, can shed enough light to shift a perspective. Can you recall a time when someone brought lightheartedness to your gloomy mood? That was a lightworker in action. You naturally shifted in the light of who they are like water always finding the path of least resistance.

As a lightworker you recognize who you are in the world because you carry a light that causes you to often be open-minded and open-hearted, being compassionately with people places and situations, showing up as a bright light in the world. You light up a room. In other words, you know yourself to be that light.

The Power of YOU As Light

You know when you're around someone who's a lightworker because the light in you recognizes the light in them, and vice-versa. A lightworker knows they're a lightworker and is working the light. You can be consciously emanating light, standing in the back of a room filled with people, and those who resonate with your light will naturally be attracted to you. In that one instance that room full of people will be elevated. This is the power of light. This is the power of YOU.

When you light up in your own recognition of who you really are - Bam! Connection happens in a way that reminds you of the light that you are here to shine with and through each other. Like adding logs to a fire, the flames increase and the light glows brighter, lighting up more of the room. Likewise lightworkers recognizing each other increases the flow of light and love into our world, or into any situation. You are here to flow light for that purpose, enlightening our world.

———————

*"[connection is] the energy that exists between people
when they feel seen, heard, and valued;
when they can give and receive without judgment;
and when they derive sustenance
and strength from the relationship"*
- Brené Brown

———————

Science has now proven that we are beings of light. Research by biophysicist Dr Fritz Albert Popp at the University of Marburg in Germany, showed that our DNA emits light, and that the cells in our bodies actually use light to communicate[1]. This differs from what scientists previously believed: that chemistry was largely responsible for the communication of information between the cells and organs in our bodies. He also proposes that, not only do the cells within our own bodies use light to communicate, but also that our bodies are in constant

———————

[1] See "Is DNA The Next Internet" by Dan Eden. Online article at http://www.viewzone.com/dnax.html

communication with each other, through light. Regardless of distance, our bodies are using light to sing to one another!

---

*"We now know, today, that man is essentially
a being of light."*

- Dr. Fritz Albert Popp, biophysicist

Being a lightworker means that you resonate to the words *"you are a bright light in this world,"* even though it may not look that way to everyone. For example a homeless person can be bringing a great light into this world, sitting in a doorway on a street corner. Just like passing a child in a stroller, a passenger on a train, or while caught in traffic someone catches your eye, we all carry a light that shines through a wide variety of physical forms. There is no stereotype for a lightworker.

This brings to mind a moment when I noticed a young man, who I would often see sitting alone at an outdoor café. Sometimes he would have his head down, sleeping on his backpack. This particular day I intentionally connected eye to eye. He smiled brightly as if he was being recognized for the first time that day. As I left the café he gently approached me at my car and with a stuttering voice asked for fifty cents to take the bus home. That exchange of light in the brief glance earlier, somehow gave him a sign that I was someone he could approach for his humble request.

Ponder your own life for the giving and receiving of similar 'fifty-cent' moments with the many people who have touched your world, like a laser beam through the heart. Perhaps as a doctor, lawyer, construction worker, loan officer, retail assistant, teacher, etc. Numerous rays of light of varying degrees are carried by a myriad of beings on this planet, creating the kaleidoscope of humanity.

Taking The High Road

Having the capacity to lighten up situations, allows a lightworker undercover to recognize opportunities to 'take the high road,' in an argument or misunderstanding. Take a work scenario for example, where employees are in a lunch room and gossip is happening. An undercover lightworker will be the one who stands for the person being talked about, and suggests the conversation not continue until the person is there to defend themselves.

You, who are recognizing yourself while reading this, can most likely at this point see yourself having taken the high road many times in your life through thought, deed and action. This will lighten our world from the many shadow aspects being played out consciously and unconsciously in our world right now.

A Slice of Light Can Illuminate Fear

Fear, being one of the darkest feelings (often used for control), is prevalent in society right now. You, as a lightworker, can be the light where fear cannot remain. Just like walking into a dark room with a flashlight that shifts the darkness, a single ray of light has an effect beyond description. Being undercover means you're likely placed with people and situations that need the most light. Yet it can be in the tiniest micro-moments, that a slice of YOUR light can illuminate, shifting the shadow forever. Again, this is the power of YOU in your light.

In the collective of humanity, every ray, shade, and shape of light is needed, to evolve human consciousness. The bully on the playground and the person being bullied are both playing out their rays of light, just as the heart-centered teacher who calms the situation is also playing out his. All contributing to the evolution of the heart, Soul, and consciousness of humanity.

"We are swimming in an ocean of light."

- Dr. Fritz Albert Popp

Being aware that the 'light of love will change the world' doesn't mean that in every moment you're lit up to 100%, because in any given moment you will be at a different point on the light spectrum. It's just that you're cognizant. You're conscious. You're aware and at choice to the degree of how, where, and when, you are bringing in light that's emanating in our world.

You are a flow-er of light, like a flower flows a scent. When we smell the scent of a flower, that flower is flowing light in the form and frequency of the scent that you're breathing in. Just as the perfume from a rose lightens you up, in the same way, we are really lighting each other up. This is one way with nature that we exchange light. You are part of nature, and nature is reflecting your light back to you. Just think of how you feel whenever you are with a beautiful sunrise or sunset, or walking along the ocean, or in a lush vibrant woodland. Nature is reflecting your light back to you, mirroring light to light, which is exponentially lightening our world. The more light, the less shadow. Some people would call that bringing heaven to earth. It really makes you think, doesn't it? *Who IS a lightworker?* ★

Chapter Two

You Are Here To Emanate Light In The World

"Light is undiminishable, eternal and omni-present.
In every religion that existed these qualities have been
recognized as divine. So that we are forced to the
conclusion that light, actual sensible light,
is indeed the direct vehicle of divinity:
it is the consciousness of God."

\- Rodney Collin

You Are Here To Emanate Light In The World

Where do lightworkers shine their light? Lightworkers shine their light everywhere because they are conscious of being a beacon of light. The more light, the more potential for a lower vibration to shift to a higher frequency of consciousness. Like turning a light on in a dark room. It's not about the doing, it's not about directing the light. It's about being aware that as you move about the world, at home, at work, as you receive all kinds of information about life and relatives and illness and world events, that you know your light can lighten that up.

It doesn't mean that you ignore something, on the contrary you actually lighten it up by how you receive it. When you receive it through the heart, when you receive it through being in empathy about the people involved in the situation, you're transforming it. Not by doing, by who you are being.

Receiving Through Your Heart

So what does it mean to 'receive through the heart?' For me, as a lightworker, I know I'm being 'used' when my heart light turns on (which is often). This is a felt sense of warmth, like a beautiful flame in the center of my heart that's creating a warm glow, which feels to me like a beautiful sense of loving and being loved. Like when you see a new puppy or a kitty or a baby, there's a warmth there and, for a brief moment in time, nothing else matters as if nothing else was more important than that connection.

That's what it feels like to me when I find myself feeling the flow of this light energy moving through me. A beautiful warm, wonderful feeling. Very non-judgmental. This is what I mean by being in empathy, and receiving through the heart. We will all have a different way of experiencing how we receive light through the heart. For me, as a high empath, it is through feeling.

I remember as a child looking through a kaleidoscope

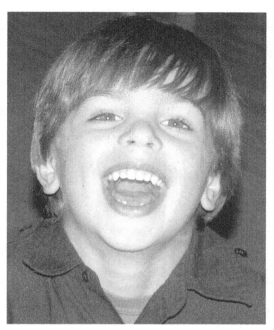

while holding it up to the light. When I first looked through that kaleidoscope all the colors were lit up, shining, and moving. In all kinds of amazing shapes and shades. That's the first time I ever recognized myself as being a being of light, because I could actually feel those rays of light as frequencies within me.

When I looked through the kaleidoscope and saw all the glass spinning then taking shape, something in me knew then, *"I'm a part of that light. I am that light!"* because I was feeling a resonance with the light. It's like when you take a crystal, a beautiful crystal, and put it in the window so prisms of rainbow light dance all over the room. You know you're a lightworker when your inner sparkle is ignited around those situations!

You know you're a lightworker when you recognize yourself as a being of light, here to lighten up our world.

Recognizing who you are as a being means 're-cognizing' that you, as a human being, are a being of light. Re-cognizing means changing your 'cognitions' (thoughts and/or ideas). Notice how your thoughts and perceptions change as you ponder some of the ideas that are in this book. You might think to yourself, *"I'm a flow-er of light? I'm starting to see the evidence of that now!"*

You Exchange Light

The light you emanate as a lightworker permeates every form of life on this earth. When you walk by a tree, when you walk by a bush, when you walk by animals, or a bee buzzes by you, or a mosquito zips by you, you're exchanging light. We all are!

We all are exchanging light just like a plant, when the light is coming in from the Sun and, in the right environment, the right conditions, all of a sudden that plant begins to flower as a result. We are like that plant. Others can flower in the environment of our light. I get all lit up, fired up, just thinking about that! How precious we are to this earth. How precious our life is on this Earth as a flow-er of light, grounding, integrating, and emanating that light for the benefit of all mankind, the Earth, and beyond.

When a mother is humming to her crying baby, the baby begins to harmonize with the mother's humming and quiets. It isn't long before there is an established frequency between mother and child and, just by humming, the baby either calms or remains calm through the mother's humming. They become cohesive. The sound of the humming and the frequency of the feeling, are all reflections of light. There are many ways of being in the light of who we are.

You As A Lightworker Undercover

So now can you see yourself as a lightworker undercover? When flowers brighten your bedside as you're recovering from an illness, it is because they are emanating a very refined frequency of light. You see them as flowers, but they're really light. You would see it in Kirlian photography. You can begin to recognize how much light is enlightening our planet (and each other) as frequencies of light are expressed through undercover actions, often unnoticed by the receiver.

You are an instrument for light, and you are here to flow a very unique frequency of light that is unlike any other. As with any instrument like a piano or guitar, the one who is playing gives it a distinct, unique, sound, tone, and rhythm. Likewise light also begins to shift in its frequency, vibration, and color, depending upon both who is flowing that light (the musician) AND who is receiving that light (the instrument).

Even though an ice-cream store may have 28 flavors from strawberry, to chocolate, to vanilla, ice cream is ice cream. When you come to realize that, you can say, *"eewww I don't like chocolate ice cream"* but at the end of the day ice cream is just ice cream. You might taste strawberry and say, *"I love this"*! It's not that the chocolate was bad, it's just a matter of preference based on your taste buds and how you're wired. Likewise, light is light. It's what flavor, shade, or shape of light that one is emanating and receiving that makes each of us unique in our expression. This uniqueness is what makes up the ever-changing kaleidoscope of humanity's light.

Humanity Is One Kaleidoscope of Light

There is one important difference between your unique light, and ice cream. Unlike ice cream, the bandwidth or oneness of humanity is more like a rainbow in that you can't separate the colors, even though there are different shades. Humanity is one kaleidoscope of light and, just like a rainbow, you can't separate the colors from the light. It's one rainbow. One kaleidoscope of humanity. So you are carrying a unique frequency of light and at the same time you are an inseparable part of the rainbow of humanity.

How Precious Your Human Life Is

What an awesome world we will be living in, when we all can see and recognize (as in re-cognize), that we are all bringing degrees of light for each other, affecting the evolution of the collective consciousness of humanity and beyond. Imagine that! We are talking about YOU. Are you starting to get how precious your human life is to all of us? Humanity is a bandwidth, and we don't go until we all go, as that bandwidth of humanity.

You as a lightworker are increasing the speed and refinement of the evolutionary light of humanity. Where in that universe can you shine your light? It starts by noticing where you already ARE that light: at the dinner table, at work, sitting at your desk, answering the phone etc. You might be getting groceries and you notice the checkout clerk has their eyes down, kind of on auto-pilot.

All of a sudden you say, "*Hello, how is it going for you today?*" the person looks up. Bam! Connection. Your eyes connect. You exchange a smile. You exchange light. And in that, there is healing. What is healing? My working definition – healing is the balancing of a system. Any system, whether it's a physical body, family, community, government, or the entire system of humanity.

"We must shift the perception we have of ourselves and see ourselves as more than just physical bodies. We need to remember that we exist on two dimensions – that of matter, the physical body and the mind, and that of energy, the spirit and the soul. Our spiritual nature comprises all."

- Carol Ritberger, "*Healing Happens: With Your Help*"

If you're still wondering as to where in the universe you can show up and shine your light, wonder no more. Everywhere! And everywhere starts right here, right now. With you. Just by you reading this book, are you aware that your frequency is elevating?

This book is infused with light. You are becoming lighter and brighter just by the transmission of these words. You are becoming more of the light that you are. You are expanding in that awareness. Can you feel it? *You are here to emanate light in the world.* ★

Chapter Three

You Are A Mirror
For Light To Reflect Light

---

*"We can walk through the darkest night
with the radiant conviction
that all things work together for the good."*

- Martin Luther King Jr.

You Are A Mirror
For Light To Reflect Light

When do lightworkers shine their light? With every word, deed, and action, a lightworker consciously knows they matter to everything coming into their awareness and beyond. Let's sit with that one for a moment.

For example when someone is sharing information with you, a neighbor, relative, co-worker etc. how are you receiving that information? Are you open-minded, open-hearted, non-judgmental, and/or compassionate? Are you hearing it polarized, such as 'us and them,' 'this and that,' 'me and you?' Or are you projecting your own stuff onto it?

For example if a co-worker is complaining to you about

the boss are you either verbally or silently in agreement? If so, you're adding to the situation. Elevating that situation would sound like, *"I hear you and for myself I agree with you however, complaining is just going to perpetuate the situation, so I really want to take a look at my role in that and how I can shift it."*

How you respond to information can result in a situation getting more tense and stressful, or getting lighter. As you pay attention you will notice it getting even lighter again as 'who you be' *is* 'being with' that person, that place, that situation. Powerful! Powerful when you really sit with the realization that you as a lightworker have this capacity at your core, just waiting to be utilized.

Fear Is The Absence of Light
Let's take a look at fear. Fear can be expressed or unexpressed. With this capacity of light, when can a lightworker have an effect with the potentially all-consuming vibration of fear? Wherever there is fear light is needed, because fear is the opposite of love and love is the highest vibration of light. Fear is the absence of light. So increasing light naturally reduces and eventually eliminates fear. So how to be with fear? When fear

is present, remain in your heart, and that is not always easy to do. Especially if you're the one feeling the fear.

You Are Not Your Fear

This is where being conscious that you are a being of light, a lightworker, a flow-er of light, is really important. Because it is in that awareness that you know *you are not that fear*. You actually can remain connected to the light of who you are and, in staying focused there, you flow a light that fear cannot remain in. This is true whether it's fear that you're experiencing inside of you, or fear that's outside of you that you're observing. You remain in the light of who you really are, a being of light that is emanating light. If we think of F.E.A.R. as *False Evidence Appearing Real*, then we can see how the 'illusion' of 'false evidence' (fear) cannot remain in the environment of light. Light is expansion, fear is contraction. When we are in the expanded state of light, we feel calm and relaxed, and there is a vibrant aliveness.

Fear is best not being ignored. Fear is best being acknowledged with the light. You can't suppress fear. You can't push it away. It's to be acknowledged with the light. Repression of fear is not putting light on the subject. So when you look directly at fear through the eyes of light, the fear-monster dissolves. Light is the antidote to the darkness of fear.

Light Calms The Frequency of Fear

It's like when a child wakes up in the night crying, *"Mommy, Mommy, I saw a monster."* You go and sit on the bed, and let him lie on your lap as you say, *"Was it a monster? Was it scary? What did it look like to you?"* and you are being with him in the light of love, as he calms in the frequency of your light. Or you turn the light on in the room, and the child calms. This is the effect light, seen or unseen, can have with fear.

The acronym for L.I.G.H.T. as *Lovelight Inspiration Gracing Humanity's Totality*, indicates a conscious lightworker's role in this fear-filled world. People are constricted by fear yet the Soul of humanity is wanting the freedom of unbounded expansion, which reflects the core of who we really are meant to be, and the light we are meant to flow on Earth.

Now let's break down this acronym of L.I.G.H.T. as *Lovelight Inspiration Gracing Humanity's Totality*:

Lovelight: Love is light, a specific frequency of light. It is the highest frequency of light and, as we shall see in the next chapter, love/light has an intelligence all of it's own. So when you bring higher light to a situation you are bringing more love, and when you bring love to a situation, you are bringing higher light.

Inspiration: The word inspire means to guide or arouse with Divine influence, or to fill with an exalting emotion[2]. When we receive more light, our vibration is raised and we are filled with the higher love of Divinity.

Gracing: When we are aware of the power of our light we are able to consciously generate a field of grace that automatically raises the consciousness of all beings within that grace-field.

Humanity: In the evolution of the planet, humanity is playing a vital role. The more we develop our capacity to flow light the more we realize humanity's role as a spaceholder for Mother Earth and all her creatures. We are like a light-filled midwife to this planet of love!

---

[2] See http://www.thefreedictionary.com/inspire

Totality: The more we live from higher light and consciousness the more we realize our oneness. We realize that all separation is an illusion and that we really are one unique ray of light in the rainbow that is the totality of our human family. Notice that in your world. Walk through the world as the light of love.

Polarized Thinking Cannot Remain

As a lightworker you are being a light in this world, especially around fear. Just a reminder, the acronym for F.E.A.R. is False Evidence Appearing REAL (for example the idea that we are separate from each other). Fear isn't 'wrong.' Love isn't 'right.' Light isn't 'right.' In the world of *unity consciousness* (that we are moving into in the new world) polarity thinking, such as right-wrong, black-white, cannot remain. Like a rainbow humanity is one bandwidth where you cannot separate the colors out. It is one rainbow. Likewise, humanity is one kaleidoscope of colors of different sizes, shapes, and shades.

This oneness is apparent in the acronym for L.I.G.H.T: *Lovelight Inspiration Gracing Humanity's Totality.* Light knows no separation. The heart knows no separation. Light moves through the world without discriminating between people, places, or situations, bathing all of nature, of which we are a part. Light just IS and fear cannot remain in the light of love.

"Love is cure.
Love is power.
Love is the magic of changes.
Love is the mirror of Divine beauty."

- Rumi

When your heartstrings are tugged at, and something just gives you a little pull in the heart, your lightworker's light turns up. Your heart light turns on. It could be when reading something in the newspaper. A recent tugging at my heart happened when seeing a picture on Facebook of a young boy in Ecuador, after a large earthquake. He was holding his head in his hands in a way that we often do when something feels too much. He had his head pressed against a chain link fence and an older man had a gentle hand on his shoulder. To me it appears as though this man was not trying to change the situation: he was simply 'being with' this young boy, as life was too much for him in that moment. This older man was a lightworker as I could see that he was allowing this young man to be in the truth of his feelings, and was simply 'being with' him through it. This is a most beneficial way to be with anyone in distress.

Sitting with that picture I felt love and compassion for all of us who have gone through our own version of life's traumas, terror, and fear. Simply having the capacity to be able to be with anything in the light of love is powerful. The most important piece is 'being with' your Self. Being with yourself, in it. Don't let 'it' pull you away from *you* because YOU are the light that is needed in the situation. You can deal with anything when you are in the light of love.

"Recognizing that everything from the DNA of our bodies to the success of our relationships and the peace of our world is based in what we believe, we see that the way we think of ourselves is now more important than ever."

- Gregg Braden, *"The Spontaneous Healing of Belief: Shattering the Paradigm of False Limits"*

There is a lack of light in the world caused by the illusion of separation and our perceived disconnection from the light of our conscious awareness. As a result fear and disconnection are the root cause of the biggest problems on our planet right now. This is why now is the time for you to really claim your role as a lightworker. To own that. To see that for yourself. To see and know for yourself that you can and DO make a difference, by *who you BE.* When you can recognize yourself as an undercover lightworker, a being of light, you will find yourself acknowledging the light in others that you see. This is the very act that will awaken even more light in lightworkers who may be blinded by their own light, and can't see who they are being reflected back to them in the world. We all have a blind spot and this is why you reflecting their light back to them is vital, when shadows are being acted out in the world. *You are a mirror for light to reflect light.* ★

Chapter Four

Your Unique Light

---

*"There is a universal, intelligent, life force
that exists within everyone and everything.
It resides within each one of us as a deep wisdom,
an inner knowing."*

- Shakti Gawain

Your Unique Light

Why do lightworkers shine their light? It's very simple, because you were born to! It's the reason you're here. You carry a very unique ray, a unique shade, a unique shape, of light that is making an essential contribution to the kaleidoscope of humanity. Like a hologram, each tiny part is in the whole, and the whole is in each tiny part. If one piece is missing it's missing in the wholeness of all of us, in the unifying of all of us. This is how essential your unique light of love is to the whole. Love is the unifier. Love is what brings us together in the oneness of who we are in the totality of our humanity.

Pick any sport, soccer for example, every single player on the team has a part, as does every single individual sitting in a stadium of 20,000 people. It is one event happening, as a co-creation. Every single individual in that stadium is a 'player' sharing their light, and the intelligent light is having a 'conversation' (so to speak) that is expressed as the game playing out.

In chapter one we mentioned research conducted by biophysicist Dr Fritz-Albert Popp in Germany, where he showed that our cells have the ability to communicate through light. The cells in our bodies are always in communication with each other. Your cells are in constant conversation with each other, and with other people's cells. So all the people at the soccer stadium, including the team and the fans, are in energetic communication. The whole game is one huge energetic conversation, exchanging light, as in the kaleidoscope of humanity. See how you're getting that visual even more now? This gives new meaning to team spirit!

"Our human potential is far greater than we can possibly imagine and is intrinsically linked to what is unfolding within us at a cellular level. Each and every one of the trillions of cells within our amazing bodies has the ability to hold and utilize light in the form of bio photons, which are subatomic particles of light.

When a cell is illuminated the DNA within that cell is also illuminated, giving us access to the universal wisdom that is held within its matrix. By matching our microcosm (the cell) with the macrocosm (the universal energies) we begin to unlock our true nature and realize our potential for greatness."

- Barbara Wren, *"Cellular Awakening: How Your Body Holds and Creates Light"*

It's important to recognize the many ways that you ground and integrate light. At the soccer game everyone cheering for their team, the intermission band playing the music, the players high-fiving and acknowledging each other, the singing of the national anthem, these are just some of the ways that grounding and integrating light is happening. Each individual is integrating the light uniquely based on how they flow their own light. Some by clapping, some singing, some high-fiving, it's all light being experienced, grounded, and integrated, through each individual expression.

We can look at a similar scenario with a symphony and the audience listening to a beautiful orchestration of music that's also an expression of light being grounded and integrated by the people, just like the instruments being played. Think of the roots of a tree growing into the earth, grounding the light from above and integrating that light with the earth. Each of us is doing the same in our own unique way, whether as a painter, an artist, a singer, a construction worker, a gardener, or a retail clerk etc. we are moving the light through our body vehicle and grounding and integrating it in a myriad of ways.

Light Is Intelligent Consciousness

We are L.I.G.H.T, *Lovelight Inspiration Gracing Humanity's Totality*. Light is everything. In a sense, even darkness is light. Light is the intelligent consciousness from which everything arises. Light, in its subtlest form, is the light of awareness and YOU are that awareness. So when you bring your awareness to darkness, even darkness really IS light. That's one to ponder!

So why is it important to ground and integrate light? Because that's what brings each essential ray of light down to Earth and anchors it. Without you grounding and integrating that light, your unique ray would be missing and the whole of existence would be like a jigsaw puzzle with a missing piece. It's like if you sing in a choir, your voice is noticeably missing when you don't sing because you are an essential part of the overall sound of the choir. Feel your light. Your unique light. Even if you can't label it or name it, feel it. Allow yourself to consciously feel it. Every unique ray is needed. Every unique voice is needed in the symphony of humanity, which is a symphony of light. It's important to all of us that you ground and integrate YOUR light to raise the vibration of Earth, which elevates human consciousness and beyond.

Clearing Energy

Clearing energy is also important. For example, if the game is over in that stadium and everyone's gone home, you could walk into that stadium and feel a palpable energy remaining, radiating, that would elevate your energy. Everywhere we go we leave a trail of energy. I know you know this for yourself. You can walk into a room, and you didn't know there was an argument in that room before you got there, and you just feel 'off.' Like walking into a Church after a Sunday service and you may feel 'on' inside, lit up, inspired.

This also is why it's so important to clear the energy in a room. There are many ways to do that, such as opening a window, or fanning your arms in the air. Anything to lighten up the energy, especially if it feels heavy, you want to move it. Dance through it. Think of how you feel after a shower or a walk on the beach. Your energy is elevated. So clearing energy is also just as important as grounding energy.

Lighting Up Another With Your Light

Why do lightworkers shine their light? Simply because it's who we are. It's who you are. Come to know yourself as that. One of the ways in which you can come to know yourself as that is, when you move out into the world and you're connecting with people through your eyes, through your smile, through your words, through your touch, and just by being. Watch for the reflection to come back, because that's when your light is lighting them up again. By 'being' not by doing.

This reminds me of a time in my life, going through the difficulties and the devastation of a divorce, I had been driving and crying and stopped at the toll-booth to pay the toll. As I looked up at the man, out of nowhere this gentle-eyed stranger said, *"will you marry me?"* and in that moment, the very thoughts that were causing my tears were responded to. I smiled driving away, because when he said, *"will you marry me"* he gave me the answer to my question, *"will anyone ever love me again?"* He was a lightworker being a lightworker undercover!

Lightworkers, masters of light, ambassadors of light, whatever name we use we all have a capacity to flow a higher frequency of light. It doesn't mean you're better, it's just your role in this life, like flowers flow a higher frequency over let's say a cactus. It's not a fixed, permanent, state of being, it's about your capacity to move energy. It's all about degrees of density and vibration. You're here as a channel, a vehicle, for the light to move through. You are very unique in that. I can't emphasize that enough, because it's so important for you to really embrace that idea.

Your Uniqueness IS Your Success

Once you can connect to your unique ray of light Bam! You're a star twinkling in a star-filled sky. Some people laugh at the same joke, some people don't. There's your uniqueness. It's not that the joke was good or not good, but it's what's tickling your funny bone! So really notice your uniqueness as you go through the world.

Your uniqueness IS your success in life. The more connected you are to your uniqueness, the more you will polish and shine the unique ray of light that is you. The more you're plugged in to what is unique about you, the more you will vibrate to that, and success sits in that uniqueness. For example, an arthritic woman may have difficulty making herself a cup of tea, but as soon as she sits down at her piano her fingers flow gracefully across the keyboard, because she is in her joy. Likewise the more you are connected to your joy, the more you will flow your light into what you are uniquely here to do in this life, and that is where you will succeed. It's always your uniqueness that brings success. Yes! *Your unique light.* ★

Chapter Five

The Kaleidoscope of Humanity's Light

"Our prime purpose in this life is to help others.
And if you can't help them, at least don't hurt them.
This is my simple religion. There is no need for temples;
no need for complicated philosophy. Our own brain, our
own heart is our temple; the philosophy is kindness.
Be kind whenever possible. It is always possible."

- HH Dalai Lama

The Kaleidoscope of Humanity's Light

How to be a lightworker? It is most important to *be in the truth of who you are*. Speak, share, live your truth. Like a child at play be the brightest light in the room, even if you're sitting in the corner, and remember there are degrees of that brightness. There are degrees of that light.

Like any spectrum there are degrees of light showing up in different ways. So 'bright light' might not be the one that's dancing and jumping around on the play ground. A bright light could be the child that's just sitting there playing with the sand, so there are degrees of light. Be the bright light in the room, your unique version of bright light, and glow your light from the inside-out. It's from the inside out that light shines. You don't have to do anything, you don't have to go anywhere, you don't have to turn it on and turn it off, you can just connect to it and in the intelligence of that light, it just knows how to be in a situation.

You can be fully connected to your light even when you're with someone who's grieving or ill for example. Jumping up and down, being hysterical, laughing and giggling wouldn't be appropriate. If you're actions are quieter that doesn't change the intensity of the light. It just changes the way the light is being expressed. Really notice that in your life. Be aware of what happens around you when you're connected to your light, when you're connected to that Source energy, that essence, that core of who you are.

"We are learning the larger attribute that encompasses our spiritual beings. To put it simply, what we are really here to learn is the Art of Mastery itself. The definition of Mastery is finding positive uses for all energy in all situations. When we attain this, we will finally remember our true power as Creators."

- Steve Rother, *"Spiritual Psychology: The Twelve Primary Life Lessons"*

Notice when you are connected to your core, people are going to want to connect with you, because they can feel the light that's emanating from you. Notice the uniqueness of you in being an expression of Source energy within the kaleidoscope of humanity, because if we're all the same, if we were all alike, where would the kaleidoscope be? So especially pay attention to what shape, what tone, what shade, you are because in that recognition, your light grows brighter.

Igniting Each Other

My heart goes to the new children coming into the world who have an innate sense of justice, and can sense when things are not harmonious in a situation. I see evidence of that many times in the school environment of my grandchildren. A recent event happened where an older boy punched my grandson in the arm four times in succession. The group of boys were playing basketball and one of the schoolmates of the older boy came over and said, *"leave him alone"* adding, *"that's not going to happen in the team spirit of this game so you're benched unless you change that behavior."*

As my grandson told me this story his eyes were lit up as he said, *"that boy stood up for me, and made me feel really good. I will do that for other people!"* That's an example of a lightworker igniting another lightworker's light. Our light truly can be contagious in this world, no matter what age we are.

The New Children

Speaking of the new children, have you noticed they carry a light that does not like to conform or be controlled? It's as if they can see right through you, or right through a situation, especially when there's an attitude of authority over them. They respond really well when given the much-needed space to find their own way to an end result. In the education system the new children need new ways of being taught because they learn differently. Because these children bring a fresh perspective, I believe they are here to teach us how outdated the old ways are.

With new eyes, open hearts and open minds, these new children will guide us to implementing innovative creative ways of fostering the unique gifts of intelligence they bring. This will take form and shape in every arena academically, as well as the arts, through the light of their being. They range in ages from unborn to adults who are the early way-showers.

If we really step back, so that we have a broader view, we can see that much of what has been created in the world has come from a narrow, polarized, focus. This was fine in the past, but will not support a future for these very deeply expanded human beings who know how divided and separate we are. Yet they live in, and bring for us, unity consciousness. We are one big human family of light.

The Early Way-Showers

There are millions of early way-shower lightworkers who are in their 40's, 50's, 60's and 70's, who brought in and grounded the unique early rays of light, which paved the way for the others to come later. Like a beam, or a shaft of light, these early lightworker way-showers have embraced humanity and graced the shadow aspects of human beings in a myriad of ways, working in this world in all walks of life as lightworkers undercover.

Animals, children and strangers, often do a double-take when they pass by to look into the eyes of these early way-showers. They may even turn back to look again, and again. This is evidence of their presence and of the light emanating from their DNA. Can you recall this for yourself? Have you noticed this about other people when you are with them?

Something noteworthy is going on. I personally have had this experience many times in my own life, and have also noticed it with other people. So watch for the refined light of the new children. They're everywhere, in every socio-economic background, extending to the far-reaching corners of the world, as are the early ones on the planet. We'll be talking more about the light of the new children in chapter eleven.

Isn't it comforting to know, in spite of how things may appear, that there is something greater going on? The symphony of life is orchestrating and calibrating the greater picture, right before our eyes, through us as individuals, in the collective of humanity. How good it feels to think that there is a grid of light, a matrix, surrounding all of us in the light of who we are, which is *the kaleidoscope of humanity's light.* ★

Chapter Six

Harmonizing The Symphony of Humanity Through Light

"One day you will ask me which is more important?
My life or yours? I will say mine and you will walk away
not knowing that you are my life."

- Kahlil Gibran

Harmonizing The Symphony of Humanity Through Light

What does a lightworker do in the world? Think about it for a moment. As a lightworker you realize it's not *what* you do. Just like a street lamp or a lighthouse guides the ships, simply by *being* the lighthouse or simply by *being* the street light. Likewise, you realize it's not what you *do*, it's who you *be* that makes the biggest difference in our world. Who YOU be.

You don't need to direct the light, simply *be* the light. When you're lit up and connected to your core essence, every cell in your body is excited because you are flowing Source energy through the uniqueness of you, and that is emanating out in the world. Not a lot of *doing* needed. It's the being. Being that bright light in the room like a child at play. It's about *bringing the being to the doing*.

Reacting versus Responding

Being that light naturally elevates a situation. Maybe Uncle Harry is arguing politics at the dinner table, or there's a confrontation going on in your neighborhood, or a tragedy that you're hearing about on the news, and the other people in the room are reacting. You can respond, rather than react. Responding would sound like, *"I really feel for those people."* Reacting would be, *"I can't believe those murderers are at it again!"* Responding sounds like, *"I can really feel those people. I feel empathy for those people."* When you hear about harmless victims, and you ask yourself, *"Who can I be as I receive this information?"* that would be you as a lightworker realizing it's not what you *do,* but it's who you are *being* in response to the news, that makes the greatest difference in the world. The world is right in your living room, right in your family room listening to that news, listening to Uncle Harry at the dinner table as he goes on about politics… again!

Just be in your light and that will emanate out and shift the vibration in the room. You are consciously emanating love and light, and the more aware you are of doing that, the brighter your light will become. That is really what we are all up to as lightworkers: consciously becoming more light in the awareness that we are that light.

Uncle Harry's frustrated complaining about politics cannot remain for long, in the soft eyes and smile of your silent listening. What's speaking here is your smile and your soft sparkly eyes that are sharing and exchanging light with your (now) beloved Uncle Harry!

Your Light Makes A Difference

As a lightworker you know that your light makes a difference. Everything you think, everything you say, everything you do, and how you perceive the world matters because you are emanating light in all that you think, all that you say, and all that you do, which has the power to shift the perceptions of others. For example a friend once said to me, *"I have learned a lot about love by watching you interact with people out and about. I never knew that, that was love."*

"If there is light in the Soul,
there will be beauty in the person.

If there is beauty in the person,
there will be harmony in the house.

If there is harmony in the house,
there will be order in the nation.

If there is order in the nation,
there will be peace in the world."

- Chinese Proverb

So let's look a little bit more at what a lightworker undercover might be offering in a variety of situations. Eyes and ears wide open to see or hear any opportunity to lighten up and elevate a situation where lower vibrations are being expressed. Not that the lower vibrations are wrong, in a world that has been learning through polarity, a lightworker can just see and sense, know and feel when to offer a suggestion or invite a new idea that shifts and elevates an action.

Lightworkers undercover, whether wearing business suits, workout outfits, soldier's uniforms or monk's robes, are all perfectly placed, to share their light in ways that will most likely never be seen or acknowledged by others. In some way this is the perfect plan, because if lightworkers banded together and only hung out with other lightworkers, how could they do their work in the world? Which is, to shine their light in the shadows.

A maid that comes in and cleans your hotel room and is happily humming while she's working, is raising the vibration in that room and you may wonder why you slept so good in your bed at the hotel that night, such a long way from home. The grocery employee in the vegetable department, so delighted organizing all the colorful fruit and vegetables, so happy and proud at the way he is displaying them, is shifting the frequency of every produce to be eaten by the customers. These are lightworkers undercover.

Recognizing Yourself As A Lightworker

My nine-year old grandson opened a door for a woman in an electric wheelchair. As he held the door while she drove through, she acknowledged him saying *"thank you."* In his young, innocent, truth, in the light of who he is, he said, *"no worries, I did it for me."* As strange as that may sound, that is a nine-year old lightworker in action. In his truth. In experiencing himself opening and holding the door for that person, he was becoming more acquainted with his own light.

So what do I mean by that? He was *being present with himself*, and noticing his own *being*, through his own experience. He was noticing his own essence, and that lit him up. He was self-aware in that moment. This is how we recognize and acknowledge ourselves as lightworkers. The evidence of his self-recognition was his dimpled smile and the twinkle in his eye! It's in that self-awareness that we grow deeper and expand who we really be as light beings, sourcing and radiating our light in this world.

It's Your Job To Give Your Life Meaning

One of the most important ways that we consistently recognize and acknowledge ourselves as lightworkers is by giving our lives meaning. When we give meaning to something is casts a frame around our actions that ensures we always focus our everyday actions in alignment with our highest intentions.

Psychoenergetic scientist Dr William Tiller[3] explains how

---

[3] Dr William Tiller speaking on Quantum Alchemy Radio Show #33 "Science and Spirituality: The Perfect Union." See http://anyasophiamann.com/quantum-alchemy/live-coaching/

our brain prioritizes how information is to be processed. According to Dr Tiller our brain will process (and we will grow in terms of our consciousness) the information that we feel is most meaningful. Anything else is basically 'dumped.' So if we really want to stay on track, in terms of consistently recognizing our own light, and flowing our light into the world, *we need to give our lives meaning*, and one of the best ways to do that, is to really take on and embody our role as lightworkers!

When we recognize our own light a kind of permission is given to be that light even more fully, because *being* that light feels really, really good! Everything is energy. We are 'Source-erers' of Source energy and when we flow that, we light up as the beings of light that we are. Like children at play we can dance in our own light bringing beautiful music to our world and *harmonizing the symphony of humanity through light.* ★

Chapter Seven

Live In Love With The Light of You

"Being a candle is not easy;
in order to give light one must burn first."

- Rumi

Live In Love With The Light of You

I have coached lightworkers all my life, it is a passion. I have a passion for lightworkers because I know lightworkers are lighting up this world, bringing new light to dark corners, as people act out shadow aspects in a wide range of expressions. The difference that bringing more light to this planet makes is beyond measure. It's effect will be seen in the tremendous shifts in the collective consciousness of humanity, as each individual's decisions and actions align more fully with the highest good of all.

In coaching lightworkers I am honored to witness their unfolding process of self-awareness and self-recognition. It is beautiful to be witness to someone recognizing their light. I thought it would be beneficial to share this example of a recent conversation with a client, so you can also witness this process.

Kate is a lightworker undercover in a significant role in a health care profession, who touches many people's lives with her heart and her hands. My intention in sharing this coaching conversation is to highlight for you just how much one of us can support another person in coming into clarity.

Even though it may feel like it's slow, it is a coaching conversation and so, unlike a consulting situation where I would be advising, when coaching I am allowing enough space for the person to 'get it' themselves. Because, when they do there is vitally important *self-recognition* and ownership in what they get. And that leads to greater self-awareness. This dialogue may be helpful to you, increasing your self-awareness, as you recognize *yourself* as a lightworker in *your* world, just like it was for Kate.

Coaching Conversation:

Anya: Hi Kate (not her real name), it's my pleasure to support you with the questions that arose out of the seminar.

[Kate's questions followed a seminar that we had attended entitled *"Ambassadors of Light"*[4]]

Kate: *One of the things that I think is so hard for me to believe is, "Ambassador of Light" seems like such a major important role to play. I don't really see myself as anyone different or special in anyway.*

Anya: That's good! That's good. What is your question?

Kate: *Being this Ambassador of Light and helping to set this grid[5] of light just seems like it's a really big job, and it's hard for me to understand how I'm that person to play that role. Can you shed any light on that?*

Anya: I deeply hear the place you're coming from in asking that question, Kate. When you experienced yourself on a great day, on a day when you were lit up, was there anyone doing anything or were you just being?

---

[4] *"Ambassadors of Light"* was an online program available at http://Paths2Empowerment.com

[5] In this particular seminar the focus was on activating a healing grid of light around the planet.

Kate: [long pause] *I was just being.*

Anya: Absolutely! Is there anything special that you have to
         do to just really be lit up, and BE?

Kate: [giggling] *NO!*

Anya: YES! It's when we let our mind get in the way, or our
         ego gets in the way, that we think we have to do
         something. You don't have to do anything, we are all
         born to be the unique ray of light that we are on the
         planet. The same is in terms of lighting up the grid.
         Lighting up the grid is YOU being the light of love that
         you are. What I'm hearing, that could possibly be
         underneath your question, is: *"Who am I to be an
         ambassador of light?"* Only *you* can give yourself
         permission to be *who you are.* Which already IS.

Kate: *Thank you.*

Anya: Can you deny that? Right? Now give me a scene that
         brings you great joy, and by joy I don't mean the
         jumping up and down joy, just how your heart feels

with something in nature. Describe it to me.

Kate: *When I see a sunset, when I'm sailing on the water, I have that feeling.*

Anya: Bring me there, bring me there. Tell me about it. What are you seeing? What are you feeling?

Kate: *Quietness, a connection of peace. Like part of a whole, in that expansion, I feel connected. I feel that connection to a feeling that feels like home.*

Anya: Were you doing anything?

Kate: *No, nothing.*

Anya: It is already there. Even right now, Kate, in the energy exchange of us having this conversation the grid is lighting up, and in that matrix of light we too are being lit up.

Kate: *Again, I feel that peace and I feel the calmness just with our conversation.*

Anya: No 'doing' to be done!

Kate: [laughing] *No!*

Anya: 'Being' to be! You already *be* the light and that
        stillness, that calm, as I'm looking at the sunset here
        out my window, that nature, is just reminding us that
        we *are* that light. Especially when we are connected to
        our being, and then, in that, we *bring the 'being' to the
        'doing.'* It changes everything. What was underneath
        your question is, *"Who am I to be an Ambassador of
        Light?"* It's pretty simple, you just claim *that which
        you already are*, and when you connect to it, it's
        undeniable.

[Here Kate is being invited to *give it meaning*. This is
important for the growth of our consciousness, as we
mentioned in the work of Dr William Tiller in chapter six.]

Kate: *Sure. I see that for myself now. Thanks.*

Anya: Because to try and deny it, it would be like putting a lid on something that you can't put a lid on. Does that make sense?

Kate: *It does, because that's why I felt so called to be a part of this seminar. It was something that I knew I had to do.*

Anya: Is that true, did you have to do it?

Kate: [giggling again] *No, I chose to do it.*

Anya: Yes! Yes!

Kate: *I chose to do it because it was very important for me to be a part of that.*

Anya: You were being called up into who you *already are,* that unique ray of light that you were really born to be. Don't let me tell you that, come to recognize that for yourself. There's a whole lot of people being called up right now to really shine their light into the world. Did you have another question?

Kate: *I did. When I first listened to the seminar it was so*

impressive and had such an effect on me. I was just
totally there, like totally connected. I really did get it at
such a deep level. I watched the recording several
times after that. Each time I got a different perspective,
but it didn't have the same strong impact like it did the
first time. Is that because I integrated the information,
or is it that I've seen it in a different way and I'm not
having the same connection?

Anya: Yes, it feels as though you integrated with it. The first
time that you saw it, you were just lit up and resonating
with everything. The second time that you heard it, you
were integrating what you were resonating to. That
doesn't mean it's any less, it means that you're
harmonizing with it, attuning to it. You ARE being it.

It's like now that things are shifting on the planet, the
connection is different. It feels as though at times
you're not connected, yet how could you not be? We
always are. It's just that we're feeling it differently, and
so it feels like we're not connected.

Kate: *Okay … I can see that.*

Anya: Right. The connection was palpable, you were feeling it in every cell of your body and now you're integrated with it, you're resonating to it. It may not feel as exciting and stimulating, but that does not mean that you're not connected.

Kate: *I can feel it.*

Anya: Yes. That's right.

Kate: *I feel that deep inner connection and it's an amazing experience.*

Anya: When you go out and about in your world, and you're connected, do you notice people naturally connect to you? Strangers will just come by and look at you, or look into your eyes, or ask you a question, or babies in carriages will turn around and look at you, and give a second look. They look like that because they're seeing, feeling, and resonating to, your deep inner connection to Source. The outside world reflects that connection back to you, and it's that deep connection to Source that *you* are really starting to recognize and acknowledge.

Kate: *That used to happen every once in a while [strangers looking and connecting], now it happens daily. It's amazing. I was at the hair salon and people there were asking me all kinds of questions that I was answering, and they resonated so much to what I was saying that they commented, "I think we should be paying you!"*

Anya: That's the integration and now that's getting reflected back to you. We get an initial high of like, *"Oh my god this is it!"* Can you recall the times when you would read a spiritual book, and it's a real page turner? It really resonated and then one day you pick it up and it just doesn't feel the same. That doesn't mean it isn't the same. It's just that now you are that which you've resonated to. A book reminded you, a movie reminded you, a video reminded you, and now you *are* it. It *is* you.

Kate: *That's a great way of looking at it. Thank you.*

Anya: It's like eating a peanut butter and jelly sandwich and then you're like, *"Oh, I wish I could have my sandwich, where'd it go?"* You've ingested it. You are now the peanut butter and jelly sandwich! It has become a part of you, vibrationally. It's changed shape and form, and it's digesting and integrating through your system, but you're like, *"My peanut butter and jelly sandwich is gone."* No, it isn't. You've integrated with it, right?

Kate: [laughing] *That's a great analogy!*

Anya: [pause] You're not alone in that, Kate, you're not alone in thinking that it's gone. A lot of people are having that experience. If anything, it's quite the opposite, you're more in alignment and more integrated with it. You ARE the light of you. Don't let me tell you that, can you feel it?

Kate: *Yes, very much so. Thank you.*

Anya: I can feel that resonance in you right now, and I appreciate your questions.

Kate: *Thank you, Anya.*

Anya: Thank you, Kate. You're very welcome, it's my great
        pleasure.

Reflection

I want to reflect for a moment here on that dialogue with Kate.
It was quite an opportunity for me to be able to be with her in
that way. I believe the questions she asked represent the voice
of many lightworkers. To feel, to have that feeling of, *"Who
am I to be an Ambassador of Light?"* That was really powerful.
That was Kate voicing what was true for her, in coming
forward with that question. I trust that she represents a good
portion of the collective consciousness of all of us. Thank you
for asking that, Kate. I totally appreciate where you were in
that. Isn't it fun to find out you don't have to do anything, you
don't have to become anything? You just need to recognize you
already are that, a being of light. Becoming conscious of that is
the point of power, which changes how you flow your energy
in the world.

When Kate got so excited and lit up the first time she saw

that seminar, it was because she was recognizing and resonating to her light. It didn't feel the same the second or third time, because she had integrated it. She was already attuning with the energy, aligning with the energy, and allowing her light to just shine through without resistance. In the emanation of that light you don't experience those initial feelings again, because once integration has happened you merge with the energy and are now resonating to that frequency. So there's nothing to feel. It becomes you. You become it. Like the peanut butter and jelly sandwich example in my conversation with Kate.

So in the revealing question, *"who am I to be an Ambassador of Light?"* You can clearly see traces of the points raised in this well-known quote from Marianne Williamson:

"Our deepest fear is not that we are inadequate. Our deepest fear is that we are powerful beyond measure. It is our light, not our darkness that most frightens us. We ask ourselves, 'Who am I to be brilliant, gorgeous, talented, fabulous?' Actually, who are you not to be? You are a child of God. Your playing small does not serve the world.

There is nothing enlightened about shrinking so that other people won't feel insecure around you. We are all meant to shine, as children do. We were born to make manifest the glory of God that is within us. It's not just in some of us; it's in everyone. And as we let our own light shine, we unconsciously give other people permission to do the same. As we are liberated from our own fear, our presence automatically liberates others."

- Marianne Williamson

———————————————

For all the 'Kates' in the world wondering your version of *"who am I to be a lightworker?"* allow my conversation with you through this book to give yourself permission, as only YOU can do, to activate your dimmer switch and shine your unique ray of light appropriately to what feels good for you.

My wish for you is to be aware of the light that you are and, in that, let the lightness of your being illuminate your path in this world, giving all of us permission to do the same. *Live in love with the light of you.* ★

Chapter Eight

Feeling The Power of Your Light Source

"It is love alone that leads to right action.
What brings order in the world is to love
and let love do what it will."

\- Jiddu Krishnamurti

Feeling The Power of Your Light Source

In this chapter we're going to look at how you can shift frequencies of light in different situations. Feeling the power of your light source is all about paying attention to what you are feeling. Your feelings are your guidance system. I cannot stress enough the importance of getting acquainted with the messages being carried through your feelings. Bringing into practice this one idea can change your life by simply paying attention to what you are feeling. Those feelings can be felt on a spectrum: everything from good to not so good, and every gradation in between.

Psychiatrist, author and mystic Dr. David R. Hawkins mapped out this spectrum of feelings as part of a *map of human consciousness*[6] in which he used kinesiology to assign a number to specific emotional states so that we could see that they range along a spectrum just like notes on the musical scale. For example, for denser emotional states like guilt and shame he gave a figure of 20 or 30 and for lighter emotional states like courage he gave 200, and peace 600. The range was from 20 to 1000 reflecting the full experience of human emotion.

Pay Attention To Your Feelings

In this moment, for yourself, just allow yourself to say the word guilt or shame. Notice how your body feels. Next think of the word courage. Notice how your body feels. Now think about the state of peace of mind and again, notice how your body feels, and where the energy is lighter or denser, and where it is flowing or not flowing.

A great way to begin this is to simply pay attention to your hands or feet, and notice the energy flow there. You put your attention there, until you notice what you notice. It can be different for everybody: it can feel like prickly pins and

---

[6] Hawkins, David R., (2014) *"Power vs Force: The Hidden Determinants of Human Behavior"* Hay House.

needles, or it can be like moving sand within your hands and feet. It will be a sensation that gets your attention. That is the beginning of becoming aware that everything is energy, and we are that energy flowing. Using this exercise you can experience for yourself how it is possible to 'navigate' your way through a spectrum from denser to lighter energy, using your feelings as your guidance system.

Feelings Are Felt Light Frequencies

Like shades of light, your feelings are 'felt' light frequencies. Different frequencies of light are experienced in your body as feelings. When the light spectrum is darker or more dense you feel it, likewise when you move to the higher end of the spectrum of light, you feel that too.

Basically your body is a barometer of light, and you can tell what shade of light you are flowing by paying attention to your feelings. For example, when you eat lighter or denser food, you can really feel the difference in your body. That can become a practice to begin raising your awareness around energy. For example a steak dinner or a vegetable salad. In reading those words, you can already feel the difference in your body's response. Just like reading a menu to choose your lunch or dinner. How do you know what to eat? Your body knows. None is right or wrong, in this case it's just about feeling the difference of the frequencies.

Sacred Food

Some foods will resonate to a higher frequency more than others, because they contain more prana or life-force energy. There is a belief from ancient yogic traditions that the more 'alive' your food is, the more it will be able to 'give life' to you. This is why ancient yogis would eat foods as close to life force as possible, such as seeds, nuts, fruit and raw vegetables.

Spiritual entrepreneur Meg Adamson spent over 3 years experimenting with raw food to create vibration shifting recipes. Her eBook *"Sacred Food"*[7] is a collection of recipes that nourish and align mind, body and Soul by using high vibration food. When you are aligned and vibrate to higher frequency everything you do is positively affected. Whether it's writing a book, a letter, creating a recipe, having a conversation, or cooking a meal, that frequency of love light is infused in what you do. Our bodies are designed to

---

[7] "Sacred Food" by Meg Adamson at https://megadamson.net/product-category/sacred-food-recipe-book/

'synchronize' with one another[8]. In other words vibration matches vibration[9]. Everyone in contact with you, or in receivership of a meal that you prepared with love, will resonate to that vibration too.

Transmitting Light And Love

As you raise your vibration, become lighter, and are able to ground and hold more higher light, then others around you are also able to do the same. Just like the words in this book are holding a vibration that you can synchronize with, as I am resonating to the space of the light of love as I write this. My fingertips on the keyboard are transmitting the energy of the heart space, from Source, that I'm in as I write this, and you receive. Your heart can feel it.

If you pay attention when, for example, maybe you don't

---

[8] Human Beings have a capacity to 'entrain' or synchronise with an external source. It has been suggested that our capacity to do so, which allows us to keep time with music in large groups, such as a tribal rhythm or dance, evolved very early in our evolutionary process as a survival mechanism See "Entrainment (Biomusicology)" on Wikipedia at: https://en.wikipedia.org/wiki/Entrainment_(biomusicology)#Evolutionary_fu nction_of_entrainment

[9] Vibration normally matches vibration, due to the process of entrainment (mentioned above). There are exceptions to this rule which we don't have the space to go into here, such as when your vibration is low and you eat high vibration food, your body will match the higher vibration. It may be truer to say that the lower vibration attunes to the higher.

feel so good about something someone said, get your attention off what they're saying, and put your attention on the feeling that you are having as a result. What you're feeling has nothing to do with them. Nothing. It has everything to do with something that your guidance system, your feelings, are pointing you to. Guiding you to. Let's say, someone is saying something and you're not feeling so good about it. Go home to you. Go inside of you. Pay attention to your feelings that are communicating something about you, to you. Stay within you. Breathe, and simply notice that you are not feeling so good about what that person said.

Your Body Is Your Subconscious Mind

Remember that what you're feeling will always be about you, because it's *your* feelings giving *you* information *about* you. In this case the person outside of you who said something is a 'benevolent messenger' awakening you to something that's in your subconscious. Neuroscientist Candace Pert said in her book *"The Molecules of Emotion,"* that your body IS your subconscious mind. The body is like an energy garden containing seeds from earlier experiences, ranging from early childhood abuse, abandonment, illness, loss of a parent, car crash, to having the best childhood experience ever. All of this sets the tone and creates the view from which you perceive the world going forward, unless and until the denser energy is cleared.

Benevolent Messengers

When these seeds are ready to ripen, the causes and conditions will come into your life in the form of a person, place, or situation, for them to become active in your conscious mind. Although it may not seem so at the time, situations that bring up strong feelings and emotions in you are part of a most precious beneficial process, whereby you can become aware of energy that is now ready to be released, for your continued evolutionary growth and expansion. Simply put, we are all, always, benevolent messengers for each other. So I remind you again, when something feels uncomfortable to you, get your attention off the other person and pay attention to what you're feeling.

This is your opportunity to put light on the subject and engage the use of your dimmer switch. Meaning simply, if you're uptight and tense and contracted about something, lighten up. There are many ways to lighten up. Lightening up can be by simply shifting your perspective a quarter of an inch, which gives you a different view of something.

Using Your Physical Body To Shift Energy

Because your physical body is a reflection of your subconscious mind you can also lighten up by using your physical body to shift your energy. For example, distinguished international speaker and teacher Peggy Phoenix Dubro describes human energy in terms of The Lattice[10], an evolutionary model of the human energy field. In her groundbreaking books and videos she offers various effective tai chi like techniques for raising your vibration and navigating the spectrum towards lighter states, using movement of your physical body.

In her DVD *"The Lattice: Reframing Your Reality"* there is an excellent sequence which shows 3-D animations of the *Universal Calibration Lattice*® (UCL) system, within the human energy anatomy, composed of fibers of light and energy. I highly recommend this visual experience to understand your energy field. Many other techniques also use the physical body to shift from denser to lighter states, such as

---

[10] "*The Lattice: Reframing Your Reality*" DVD by Peggy Phoenix Dubro.

active meditations, Qigong and various forms of yoga.

Another way to 'lighten up' is to ask yourself the question, *"What about that is about me?"* 'That' in this case, means whatever is going on outside of you. Go back home to you. Pay attention to your feelings. Are you expanding? Are you shrinking? Are you contracting? Are you starting to feel angry? Are you starting to be pissed off? Are you starting to feel unwanted, unheard, unseen, or any feeling that is a not-so-good feeling? Keep asking yourself, *"what about that is about me?"* In other words there's a message in those feelings specifically for you. The stronger the feeling, the more likely it is that a past event (seed) has been activated in your system that's now ready to be released.

Projections On The Screen of Your Life

Something else to keep in mind is that one of the greatest traps that we can get caught in is the web of other people's projections. Most people are in relationship with the person that they unconsciously create inside their head called 'you.' However it is more about them than it is about the real you. In other people's minds we are all 'made up' versions in their head. Know that you are also doing the same thing in your head, (making *them* up and then projecting the stuff in your world on to them). They then start reacting back to *their* own projections. This is where it can get tricky because then both people's defenses and protections start to come into play. Consciousness is the only hope in this situation for it to become something different. The leader in any situation will always be the one with the most presence. Being able to 'presence your own presence' is what needs to happen in those situations so that you don't get caught in the web of someone else's mental projections.

Presencing Your Own Presence

What I mean by presencing (your presence) is simply being aware of the awareness that is you. Your awareness is the clear blue sky that is not getting caught in the clouds flowing by. Your awareness is the focus that remains on the clear blue sky. That's a great analogy as a visual to begin to understand this idea.

Perception Is Reality

In being present to yourself you will realize more and more how perception *is* reality. How I perceive you, is who you become, to me. How potent is that? In relating, who's more important? You or me? Relationship is all about *me, as relates to you*. In a sense, 'me' is all that matters when it comes to you. That is the power of perception (our mental projections) to create reality.

A Relationship Is A Never-Ending Conversation

A relationship is a never-ending conversation. The one *I'm* having in my head about you is creating *my* version of you. Who you are to me, is about me. It is *my* projection. How *I* experience you, is a figment of *my* imagination. (I like you, or I don't like you.) This is a really important point to understand. My mental projection will make you be anyone I want or need you to be in that moment. So where does that leave YOU in all of this? Doing the same thing as me!

You're In Relationship With Your Projections

You are creating *your* version of me (and others) at the same time with your own mental projections. So what's really going on in any interaction is that I'm only ever in relationship with who I perceive you to be, and you're in relationship with who you perceive me (and others) to be. Until we become more aware and conscious, in the clarity of being more present.

Click The Refresh Button

A powerful technique to remember to be more present (and stop projecting onto others) is to "CLICK the REFRESH button!" Every day, with every encounter on the movie screen of your life, CLICK the REFRESH button often so that who you are perceiving the other person to be (which is creating your reality of them) is current and true.

We Are Mirrors For Each Other

Who we were yesterday is not who we are today unless you drag and drop it in! Are you getting the picture here? Can you see the roles we're playing for each other? I get to mirror you, back to you, and vice-versa! When we bring in more light and conscious awareness by being fully present, my higher view of you is also what becomes true for me, in my reality. In that clear space of higher consciousness you can show up differently. Your bad day can't act out in my space (or at least not for long). Our frequencies want to harmonize to the higher.

Click your refresh button daily for a truer 'now moment' view, giving you the space to be interacted with, for who you are today, because you may have shifted since yesterday. A shift in perception allows a new perspective which creates a

http://AnyaSophiaMann.com

new reality for us both to interact in, affecting everything![11]

The Witness / Observer

As you continue this practice, you will begin to notice a place within you, from where you can see that what's happening outside of you is not about you. Let's give another name to that place: the witness or observer. The one who has no judgment about anything and is just witnessing, noticing. That's the place I'm referring to. In the place of being the witness you simply notice the feeling of 'not so good.' Just notice what you notice, and that's enough for a shift to happen.

Keep your attention on the place that's noticing (witness/observer), because that place then becomes a space. A spaciousness. Giving you the capacity to 'be with what is.' Whatever 'is' (the person at the table saying not nice things and you're not feeling so good about it), it gives you the capacity to *be* with 'what is.' Remember the beautiful example of the street light just emanating light. It doesn't judge anything that is going on in the illumination of that light. It doesn't turn itself on and off depending upon what's going on! It could be a

---

[11] Watch this exercise in the video "*YOU From A Different View*" at
http://AnyaSophiaMann.com

street-fight, it could be lovers hugging and kissing, it could be children playing, or a car crash, whatever is going on the light is just being the light, emanating light.

The Capacity To Be With What IS

In the capacity to *'be with what is'*, you are creating the space for it to dissipate because you are giving no energy to it. In other words, you are not engaging with it on a manifesting level. Giving energy to the situation would sound like, *"Why are you saying that? I don't feel good when you say that"*, as opposed to having the capacity to 'be' the space. When you just 'be' with what is you expand. In the space of your expansion the situation can dissipate, the contraction can dissipate. In other words, it no longer matters to you. It no longer matters. It's just there in the room, there in the space. It no longer matters. It just *is*.

The moment you engage with something at the level in which it came into your space, you're caught like a fish on a hook that can get reeled in. If you meet it at that level, you're engaged with it and your energy will match it. So if you were feeling courageous and vibrating at 200, if you match someone's shame at 20, your vibration will drop from 200 to 20. Your light will dim. Move back to the place where you have the capacity to *'be with what is'*, and you will lighten up again. Create space, and in the expansion of you, you are able to just 'be with it' without engaging. Then something amazing happens. It begins to dissipate. You no longer have interest in it. Like a cloud moving and changing shape in your clear blue sky. It comes. It goes. No attachment.

It doesn't mean that you won't still have that feeling. Now that you have your attention off the scenario, you could still have the feeling of it. Now that you're away from that scenario, or it's dissipated, or you don't care about it anymore (in a very positive way), you allow your energy to come back to you, but you still may have that feeling. That's when you can go a little bit deeper.

Love Is The Highest Frequency of Light

As you sit with the feeling (which is your guidance system communicating with you) there is an opportunity for you to love you, in that feeling. Meaning, you go into the feeling. You don't separate from it. What I mean by that is when you bring love to it, that love unifies, it does not separate. As was mentioned earlier love is the highest frequency of light. So explore where you can love yourself with that not so good feeling that you're simply noticing (not getting caught in). If you blame something (or someone) outside of you for that feeling, that is *s e p a r a t i o n*. That is disconnection from your essence, from your core. Remember, the root cause of many problems in this world is disconnection.

Where Can You Love You?

Connect back in. Where can you love you in that feeling? Imagine your feelings are a small child, three years old, maybe feeling hurt by what another child said to them. How would you be with that child who is hurt? You'd be that love for that child. How can you love yourself through your feelings as if they were a three-year-old child feeling that same feeling? That's taking the light of you just a little bit deeper into your world.

Now you're really paying attention to bringing love, the ultimate 'unifier.' The higher light of love has the vibration of unifying. When you bring love, instead of separating from your feelings, you're joining with them. You're loving them. You're bringing love to them, which is increasing. In doing so, you're expanding your capacity to *'be with'* even more.

When we say you no longer care, we mean it from the highest meaning that anyone could give those words, *"I don't care."* Actually, it's a beautiful place to be when something is not worthy of you giving care to it. *"I don't care,"* in this sense, is non-attachment in its highest form. You're not attached. It is a carefree-ness with compassion.

Skillful Means

It is absolutely not indifference. There is already too much of that in humanity. Does it mean you don't care about the person? No, it means you are not giving your energy to that situation. You don't care to engage in it. You may never verbalize that to the person because that can agitate the situation further. Verbalizing that to the person takes skillful means, which we don't always have the capacity to cleanly express. Especially when you're in the throes of an argument.

Is it true, as some people suggest, that what you're feeling is attracting more of it to you? It depends. If you engage in it at the level at which it came into your space, the answer is yes. When you have the capacity to be able to just be with what is, the answer is no.

The moment you notice a feeling arises inside, go home to the feeling and love it. By love it, we mean unify with it. *Be* with it. Don't become it. Notice it. Love is the unifier. *Be with* it without *becoming* it. In that spaciousness, that expansion, you will find the capacity to be with what is grow in you, more and more. You will also be able to be with more that isn't love in the world. Let's call that the shadow aspects of humanity.

Shadow Aspects

We've mentioned often how shadow aspects can get acted out, so what do we really mean by shadow aspects? Shadow aspects, in this sense, means the aspects of human behavior that can come as a result of the lower end of the spectrum of feelings. So when we talk about shadow aspects being acted out, we're really talking about actions that can result from lower spectrum feelings such as fear, guilt, shame, jealousy, anxiety, blame, hate etc. These lower spectrum feelings, when we are disconnected from them (and unaware), are what causes us to project onto others. When you are able to simply be with someone who is experiencing such feelings, it creates space for them to find the higher light within themselves, which allows their shadow aspects to dissolve.

For this to be effective, you have to be really clear that you are not harboring fear, resentment, or agitation, which would be matching their energy. For example, let's say you're driving with your partner and an argument starts. You're in an enclosed vehicle, in the passenger seat, so there's nowhere to go. What do you do? You be with it. In silence. But it can't be the kind of silence that is dense, brooding, or heavy. You have to be clear. Remember *that who they are talking to is their own projection*. They are not seeing the real you. In other words they are interacting with their version of you. You can be with it from the space of breathing light into the space, to create more spaciousness for it to resolve and dissolve. That can often be in the magic of silence.

Breathe Clear Light

You might say to the person, *"maybe it's best if I listen to you without responding just now."* Even if the person is screaming and agitated and yelling. You might hold your hand on your heart and simply breathe. Breathe clear light into the space without trying to 'do' anything. The more you can relax and be clear, the quicker the energy will dissipate in that clear space. The name of the game is to become clear enough in your life so that when these things happen (as they will, projections are happening all day long in many ways), you can energetically feel the energy coming at you, and not get caught in its path. As they say in the martial art Aikido *'step to the side and let it go by.'* The point is to not get caught in other people's projections on you. The ideal is to not get caught in it at all, if possible, and if you do get caught simply notice, and see it as another learning opportunity on your path.

Clearing Your Energy Field

Earlier (see chapter four) we spoke a bit about clearing energy in a room, and it is also important to know how to clear your own energy field, so that after an experience like this you are not carrying that energy forward into your day and the next day. If someone has been screaming and yelling at you, maybe being accusatory, and you feel bad about it, how do you clear your energy field? One method that I use myself is to 'defibrillate' (I even teach this technique to doctors and nurses)! You know how you see scenes in movies where someone has had a cardiac arrest and they come with the paddles and shout "clear"? That's a defibrillator. Well, to clear your energy field you do this by saying - C L E A R - in your mind. At the same time in your mind see your field being electrified with a clear energy that nothing can remain stuck to, like shooting light into your system. Other ways to clear your field include taking a shower, a walk in nature, water (wash your hands), music, dancing, envision wind blowing through you like the wind blowing through a tree and the leaves dropping. A fresh rainfall that you're standing naked in. These are just a few of the methods that you can create for yourself. There's no secret formula here. The point is to actually do it for yourself daily. This will also support you in seeing others more clearly.

How do you know when you are carrying the energy from prior events? Some of the ways are that thoughts of the person will keep coming into your head, or thoughts about the situation, or you will feel a feeling like you felt at the time. Or you will wake up the next day and it's still there. Those are some of the indicators that you're still carrying that energy, and you need to clear your field. C L E A R!

"When one allows oneself full expression
of what is felt at the deepest levels
of one's emotional body,
one serves to clear those blockages
and to open to the heightened sensitivities
of which one is capable.

*Stimulation of the physical senses
with conscious attunement
to their correlation with particular categories of emotion,
is a direct and highly effective way
of clearing the energies that can inhibit progress
achieved at other levels."*

- Rasha, *"Oneness: the teachings"*

———————————————

So what about you, when you find yourself acting out lower aspects as you interact in different situations? You might have the thought, *"wait a minute, if I am a lightworker how come unkind thoughts and acts are being felt and expressed by me?"* Exactly! How perfect. Of course any 'seeds' in you that are not of the light are going to be activated in the light of you.

As you become lighter, deeper, and more expanded, anything that is not that higher frequency is going to move out through the light of you. This is not a case of you are this *or* that, shadow *or* light, this is a case where *you are all of it*. It's a matter of how much consciousness you can bring to the shadow aspects that you are playing out. You don't *become* the shadow, you *be* the light, simply noticing the shadow energy that is moving through.

Light Has No Shadow

An important point to really understand, is that *light has no shadow*. When we shine a light onto a dense object, the *object* casts a shadow. The light itself has no shadow. This can be demonstrated easily by shining a light onto a candle, or a match. The solid body of the candle, the holder, and/or the matchstick will cast a shadow, but the flame clearly has no shadow. This explains why we will see shadows (ours and other people's) as our light gets brighter. It also clearly shows us that the light itself is not 'creating' those shadows!

Here's where it really gets even deeper. As you experience yourself responding to situations from within your own being, *you will come to know you*. You will come to know yourself on a new level. You will come to love yourself in a deeper, more expanded, way. That's why all of these experiences are coming into your life: so that you get to come back home and love even more, *starting with yourself*. In this way your capacity for higher love is ever expanding.

You Will Begin To Feel Yourself As Light

In other words, you are *becoming* that love, becoming that space, becoming that capacity to be love. We are beings of light and you will begin to feel yourself, as that light, emanating. If love is a unifier, and you are *'being with what is'* from the space of love, can you see how love expands your world and unifies us as a human family, as humanity? Really sit with that one. It's a lot to take in. Now, imagine that anything that happens *outside of you* is an opportunity for you to *get your attention off it and not be triggered by it*. Go back home to you and 'love' the uncomfortable feeling that is arising in you, just like you would that three year old child that was hurting.

When you have that capacity, that space of being able to

hold more light and more love, the shadow aspects of others are going to come up in the space of the light of you. Some people have the idea that you reach a certain point in life where you're just love, and off you go. It doesn't work like that. Being at that capacity to be able to love and 'be with' means exactly that. In order for you to be that, things have got to come into your space or you will not experience yourself as the light and love that you are here today.

You Are The One - In EveryONE

As you continue keeping your attention and intention on being the best 'you,' there will be a growing sense of empowerment that 'all is right in the world.' You will know that you are right where you are meant to be, doing exactly what you're meant to be doing, for everyone else, through yourself. There is a knowing that you ARE the one in everyONE. All that's needed for the healing of the whole of humanity, happens through the individual. In the beingness of higher light and love, natural adjustments will innately be made by conscious individuals, fully knowing that their words, thoughts, and actions, affect the collective heart and Soul of humanity.

The brighter your light gets, the more situations are going

to come right up into your space, in the light of you. So that you get to not react, but rather to respond by going within your own being. This creates the space for that situation to not be more energized because you are not giving any more energy to it. The greatest gift you can give our world is to flow love. When you are in that love space the shadows that are arising in it cannot and do not affect you, because you are in clear space.

There is a lot here in this chapter that warrants re-reading a second and third time as your perspective will shift each time and you will be able to hear and understand more fully with each new shift in perception. More importantly is that you actually put into practice the ideas expressed here, so that they become second nature to you, as you experience the power of your own being. As you experience that, you will really be flowing your energy for the whole of humanity, and that is what it means to be *feeling the power of your light source.* ★

Chapter Nine

Bringing The Light of Your Being To What You're Doing

"Love is the natural condition of all experience before thought has divided it into a multiplicity and diversity of objects, selves and others."

\- Rupert Spira

Bringing The Light of Your Being To What You're Doing

You know truth, as what's true for you. What's true for you IS the truth in that moment, and your truth is ever-evolving. For example as a child I remember my mother teaching me the expression, *"sticks and stones will break my bones but names will never hurt me."* I would sing that inside my head whenever other children called me names and for me that phrase was truth. To this day I know there isn't anything that anyone can say to me, or about me, that is about me. It's about them and they're entitled to their experience. Your truth is *your* truth in this moment. Your truth in the next moment. All of it is shifting as a result of you evolving. No one outside of you can really tell you anything about you. You've got to come to the experience for yourself of what's true for you, by paying attention to what resonates for you and what doesn't in any moment.

What follows is an excerpt from my radio show[12] with a live caller named "Lori." As the conversation unfolds we can see how she follows the guidance and inklings of her inner-truth in the moment, and what happens as a result, which speaks to the fact that only you can know what is really true for you. By recognizing what is true for her in the moment, Lori is able to connect to her inner-light. Through the quality of her attention, she is then able to bring more presence, more 'being-ness', to what she is doing. So in this example we can see how Lori uses the experience of her truth to connect to the light of her being, and then brings that light of awareness to what she is doing. In this way she *'brings the being to the doing.'*

Anya: Lori, have you been able to listen to the show so far or are you just calling in?

Lori: *No, no. I've been listening. I've been deeply listening.*

---

[12] Aired live on Quantum Alchemy Broadcasts - Quantum Conversation #127. Listen to the full broadcast online at http://anyasophiamann.com/quantum-alchemy/live-coaching/

Anya: Does anything resonate that you want to share?

Lori: *Yeah. Actually this call is, of course, timely but I'll share a story from yesterday. I desperately knew that I needed to get my hair done. When my oldest daughter Molly asked me why I had gray hair, I thought, "Okay. You know what? It's time I got it colored." I was really excited to do it. My husband said that he could come, and that he'd watch the kids from 5 to 7pm before he had to leave. I could just tell when I picked them up from school, "Yeah, this is going to be tricky leaving them to get my hair done."*

Sure enough when I said, "Okay, I've got to go," both of them just completely had a meltdown! Molly (age 5) was just hysterical. Normally, I would have come into that space emotionally charged but this time I just totally detached and I thought, "This is happening. This is happening right now." I didn't go into, "Okay, I am going to be late," or all that rant. I just thought to myself, "This is what's happening. Just be calm."

Anya: Beautiful.

Lori: *Then I realized, "You know what? This is where they're at. This doesn't happen a lot." For whatever reason they're both intent on coming so I'm just going to go with it. I'll bring them both with me and see what happens. It turned out that the hairdressing place, was unusually quiet. Normally, I would have been worrying about that because Molly can sit for a few hours but Lily (the youngest) can't.*

In the moment I said, "Is there somebody who could do Lily's hair?" She just ate it up! It was just hilarious watching her. This little three-year-old in this big chair! It was just hilarious. I ended up being there for two hours. It was so fun. There were a few moments where I thought, "Okay. Would she knock stuff over as the lady is blow drying my hair?" but just I let go. I let the four women in the salon be who they were. I let the kids be who they were. It was so beautiful.

As you Anya often talk about this capacity to love more, I just worked with it. Before, I would have been all anxious, but I let go of the anxiety and thought, "Okay, let's just play." Everything you spoke to was exactly what I experienced yesterday. I never would have had that capacity to expand in it had I not just allowed it to unfold.

Anya: Yes, yes, yes. Beautiful, beautiful! Now, big question coming now for you and all the listeners, so take a moment and a breath before you answer: *"Who were you being in it, Lori? Who did you come to know yourself to be, in that actual experience?"*

Lori: *Just fun, loving, open and no role. I wasn't in a role. I wasn't 'mom.' I wasn't needing everything to be right, or perfect, or look a certain way. I was just loving this energy. I just allowed everyone to be. I lost me in it all.*

Anya: One hundred percent... Yes! Well done! You took the roles off. Now, I'm going to help you a little here. You said, *"I just allowed everyone else to be."* Sit there for a moment. Really catch this one, listeners. Lori said, *"I just allowed everyone to be."* Lori... that's not your job!

Anya: You were just being the space in which everything else unfolded. It's like a children's playground. Can you imagine if the swings just started going, *"Oh god, here they come again! This one swings me too high and that one swings me too low!"* The playground just is. It just is. No judgment. The children come in as an energy. Then energy simply interacts with energy.

Lori: *So Lily sees the chair and how it starts to pump up, and I'm like, "Okay, okay." That was really a great experience for me in knowing the fine line of when to just let it be.*

Anya: Beautiful.

Lori: *What I also learned was that in that moment, there was no judgment. I was just watching. Just seeing it all unfold. Like when you said about being 'the observer.' I noticed how awesome it feels to be fully in my essence in that hair salon, fully connected to myself. Simply observing everything and not getting caught in it. I thought, 'Wow, these kids. This is their first time in a hair salon.'" It felt so good just being that relaxed, connected, person having so much fun with the kids.*

It's just like a story. It could have gone so many different ways. I realized why it's so important that I stay connected, because what I bring to every situation is so magical. I realized, "Wow! Every little encounter I have has such an impact on everybody."

Anya: Absolutely, absolutely! Now, listeners come with me, I'm going out on a limb with Lori right now, because what I heard in Lori just then, was Lori touching her 'god self.' In other words, in observing what was going on in the hair salon (which could be seen as a microcosm of earth and humanity), Lori was allowing the space of pure love to expand exponentially, increasing it's capacity to unify the room and everyone in it! As a result harmony happened. By allowing it all to play out in the playground of that hair salon, Lori, as an awakening undercover lightworker, was consciously using her presence in a higher capacity, which harmonizes the earth.

Lori: *What I also experienced, which you just helped me to put words to, was I felt the polarity. I felt fear in certain moments but I loved myself through the fear. I noticed the shift from fear to love at the time and now, hearing you explain it, I realize that's what I was doing [consciously using her presence in a higher capacity]. I was feeling the fear but I wasn't reacting to it or getting hooked in. I was noticing thoughts like, "Okay. Is Lily going to break this chair? Is Lily going to spray this water everywhere?" and just trusting. Just trusting that if I needed to step in I could handle it.*

Anya: Totally, totally. Fear is an invitation. What I mean by that is this: fear is the absence of light. So when you felt fear, that was your inner guidance system saying to you, *"Come back home. Get your attention back home, and stay as the love vibration that you are. Emanate that out into the room and watch everything just be fine."*

Lori: *Yeah. It takes such courage.*

Anya: Yes. Yes.

Lori: *I really felt it because it's out of my comfort zone to let things unfold that way. It really was foreign to me, but I just knew. I just knew inside, as a result of all of our coaching, that this experience was happening for a reason. Meanwhile, I could hear the voices play out like, "You need to go, and they need to be at home, and la la la," but I thought, "Not this time. For some reason, not this time." I just trusted that.*

Anya: Right. It was all perfect.

Lori: *Yes, I see now, it was all perfect.*

Anya: Beautiful. Beautiful! They experienced themselves exercising freewill. Children are amazing when left alone. They monitor themselves. They know when to pull back. They know when to move forward. They are amazing because children innately are following their spirits, following their guidance systems. Not in the same way we are, but children can run to the edge of a cliff and everything in their body stops. They look around and go, "Oh okay," and turn around, and go the other way. That is all innate to us as human beings

Lori, until, it gets conditioned out of us, and we stop using our natural guidance system.

Yay for you! This Mother's Day coming, you get yourself some extra flowers just to celebrate who you are becoming. Not so much as a mom, but who you are becoming in the love that you are, in the spaciousness of the capacity of being love. Love can be with anything and everything, no matter how shadow-like or dark it might appear. If it comes into your space, it's coming into your space because you are the light that's going to lighten up the shadow aspects that are being played out in that experience.

Lori: *Yeah, yeah. Thank you, Anya, for letting me share.*

Anya: Yes. Your precious little beings got to experience themselves even more deeply in who they are, which is love, just running about the playground of that hair salon, and letting other people simply love them. How gorgeous is that?

Anya: Lori, I can't think of a more beautiful situation than this one you've brought forward, for our listeners to begin to really understand some of the ideas that I've coached you on today. In that hair salon you experienced love, freedom, liberation from the chains of underlying fear that were binding you to not let the free spirited children be free spirits. Good on you. Thank you so much, Lori. Thank you for that. We all benefit by the conscious mothering that you are moving into more and more.

Lori: *Thank you.*

Anya: I appreciate and celebrate you. Love and hugs for the girls too.

Reflection

So now we will take a look at the underlying process of what was unfolding for Lori in her experience with her daughters Molly and Lily.

Lori was able to observe herself. [see chapter eight: witness/observer] She was able to notice her feelings, to notice her thoughts, and yet stay in a 'charge neutral' place where she wasn't actually engaging with any of those old thoughts and feelings. She was able to stay fully present. She was able to 'be with' what is. As her story unfolded, we could see her capacity for 'being with what is' increasing. It unfolded perfectly and is a beautiful illustration of how we, as undercover lightworkers, can lighten up situations by how we 'be with' them. Lori had the capacity to be with all of it, to move with all of the feelings that were coming, to observe and ponder, and to reflect on her experience. When any one of us does that, it really evolves us all and, as a result, the situation.

The expression 'charge neutral' is a coaching term. It's a language approach used often in coaching conversations. Simply put, charge neutral means going forward in a neutral or middle way. You're not on this side, you're not on that side. You're just staying right in the middle as you move forward. You remain neutral in a situation. It's not good, it's not bad, it just is.

Lori having her hair done, while the kids were simply being free spirited children in that environment; her husband intending to take her and mind the kids, and then it changing in the moment so they ended up going with her; that was all moving forward. Feel free to read that sentence again so that you really get the motion of *being with what is,* and the freedom of non-attachment that comes with that. Moving forward from the middle, a neutral place. In other words, she was connected to the center of her being. What I heard the most with Lori, is how she was loving, and being, with herself through it. In particular, when she said, *"But it really took courage."* Having courage is a form of *loving yourself* through something. The reward for acting on courage is, and will always be, confidence. Self-confidence. Most people think you need confidence first. It is quite the opposite: confidence is the reward for courage. Lori was being fully present to herself. In that presence there was space for something to become different and shift to a more natural state.

"The highest state of love is not a relationship at all, it is simply a state of your being. Just as trees are green, a lover is loving. They are not green for a particular person, it is not that when you come they become green. The flower goes on spreading its fragrance whether anybody comes or not, whether anybody appreciates or not."

- OSHO, Indian Mystic

Love is a unifier. It's an energy that unifies. Lori loving her way through it means she was 'being with' unifying, 'being with' what was there in front of her. The kids on the chairs, and the kids over there, and the owner, and the other operators, and this, and that. Loving, being with what it is, and not separating from it. That's the key. Don't separate, don't pull back from it. Be in the field of the love and light that you are, and allow things to unfold in the space that you're creating, by being that which you're vibrating and let everything unfold in that field.

The Most Natural Place To Be

If your attention is needed in a physical way, if you need to go support a child, or whatever, you will be there for that when it presents. But wait until it presents instead of projecting on to the situation with ideas like, *"You're going to fall off that chair. You're going to … Oh, what did I tell you? I told you, you're going to fall off the chair and you just did."* Look at your role in that. Instead of giving the space for whatever is going to unfold, you impose your ideas onto the situation, which affects the outcome. In contrast, simply 'being with what is' is not an easy place to be. However, it is the most natural and best place to be for all concerned.

Perfect is AS IS

Lori also described her experience as perfect. In my work I often use the simple yet profound expression: *perfect is … as is!* Perfect is as a result of what has gone before. For example, you run out of gas because you didn't fill up – it's perfect. Perfect is … as is, meaning this moment is perfect as a result of what has gone on before. The reason Lori's situation was perfect, was because she got to experience herself being in her natural relaxed state, and then she got to see for herself how that then allowed the children to relax into their natural state too. Perfect! Because 'perfect is as is!'

If you find yourself reacting, you are reacting to something outside of you. You no longer have the resource of YOU to be 're-sourceful' in that situation. A key to knowing that you're not 'inside of you' (in other words internally referenced[13]) is that you are reacting. It is important to be internally referenced because it is only from inside of you that

---

[13] Internally referenced means your focus is on your inner experience and you believe you have the power within you to take control, take responsibility, and make changes in your life. When someone is externally referenced they give their power over to others, blame events outside of themselves for their circumstances, and often feel powerless. In psychology the concept first originated in the theory of 'locus of control' developed by Julian B. Rotter in 1954. See more in "*Locus of Control*" on Wikipedia at https://en.wikipedia.org/wiki/Locus_of_control

you can access Source energy. Reacting is always about something outside of you. In contrast, responding is always about inside of you (accessing Source energy). You have the reSource of you. From there you have the capacity to *be in you* and respond. In contrast, when you react, something outside is pulling you *away* from you and you go into reactionary mode.

Go Back Home To YOU

When you notice something outside of you pulling you away, that's your invitation to *go back home to you* and respond to the situation from inside, where you are present to yourself. From there, you are able to *be with what is* in a very charge neutral or middle way. There's no 'this.' There's no 'that.' It's about *being with what is*.

Then, from that place, you can respond: you can walk over to the child and simply say, *"Come with mommy,"* or you can sit across the table from someone who is saying things that aren't best for the whole table and say, *"Can we change the topic?"* You are responding as opposed to reacting to what is outside of you. It's a very simple formula: reacting means too much attention outside; responding means you've brought your attention inside. That's a very simple, practical tip that allows you as an undercover lightworker to shine your light consistently in any given situation by going within, connecting to your presence, and then bringing that presence to the situation. That's what it means to *'bring the being to the doing,'* in other words, you are *bringing the light of your being to what you're doing.* ★

Chapter Ten

Shining A Light
On Lightworkers Undercover

---

*"Man is so made that when anything fires his soul,
impossibilities vanish"*

- Jean de la Fontaine

Shining A Light
On Lightworkers Undercover

In this chapter we'll take a look at some real-life examples of lightworkers undercover: who they are, and how they are impacting the world, each in their own way, by how they shine their light. In this way we will come to understand more deeply the qualities of a lightworker, and how to spot a lightworker undercover at work!

As we mentioned earlier, the definition of a lightworker that we are using in this book is:

A lightworker is a human being
emanating a unique ray of light
with a capacity to harmonize our world
through their boundless presence.

As we present the following examples we can see how lightworkers flow their light in often very subtle ways, and the impact that is having on everyone and the world around them.

How to recognize a lightworker undercover in action? There will often be a subtle quality of knowing exactly what they're doing and why. The 'why,' if you asked them, would often be answered with a simple *'because I can.'* An undercover lightworker will often never see the result of their 'infusion of light,' which points to the fact that they are not motivated by recognition. Noticing where you can make the smallest difference can have the biggest impact.

Stranger On A Plane

I was sitting on a three-hour flight about to relax into a book I had been looking forward to, when a passenger excused himself and gestured toward the window seat. I got up allowing him to go past to be seated. Soon into the flight (and into the first chapter of the book) my quiet, contemplative, almost troubled, neighbor was moving uncomfortably in his seat, obviously with something on his mind. Being highly intuitive and empathic I could feel his disturbance, and felt for him. I put my book down and broke the ice saying, *"are you a reader, have you read any good books lately?"* He looked quickly into my eyes and said, *"no I have other things on my mind."* I could feel how heavy hearted he was so I said, *"ok I won't disturb you any more."* Silence was between us for a moment and then without looking he just started talking, *"I haven't seen my father in 20 years and I am on my way to tell him I have a terminal brain tumor. I almost forget what he looks like."*

I knew at that point that the reason I was on that plane was much more than where I was going geographically. Any time I am being called up and into the light of easing the burden of another human being, I get this palpable feeling in my heart of a fullness of pure unconditional love for the person or situation. So with that feeling in my heart, my eyes glowed a soft warm light that I could feel emanating, like how we light up when we are loving someone through a tough time.

I asked him, *"Can you remember a favorite gift that you got as a child?"* he said, *"yes, my bike."*
"Who gave it to you?"
"My mother and father on my sixth birthday."
"Who taught you to ride it?"

I respectfully paused with him, simply loving him with the light in my heart that I felt, as he wiped the tear that had fallen from the corner of his eye.

Letting time go by, I asked, *"do you remember what he looked like as you were learning to ride your bike?"* He said, *"His hand. I remember his hand on my back letting go, and I turned around and saw how proud he was of me as I peddled on alone."*

Then he began to share his visual memory of what his father looked liked. He became more engaged with me as he verbalized the memory of what his dad looked like. I listened with great interest. I gently 'walked' with him as he imagined what he might say, and how his father might respond upon hearing the grave news that his son, whom he hadn't seen in twenty years, was dying. I knew that envisioning it in his own mind, and feeling the associated feelings it might bring up, would be very supportive for him. This would better prepare him for the actual moment.

I assured him that twenty years could be compressed into twenty minutes when love leads the connection. When I asked, *"did you love your bike and the connection you felt riding on it?"* he said, *"lady I don't know who you are but right now with everything in my body I 'get' it. I get what you just said and it feels like the truth. I feel like I just unloaded the heaviest burden of 'how am I gonna tell him' after all these years."*

No words were spoken again after that. I thought, *"lightworker   undercover   on   assignment: mission accomplished!"* As I exited the plane that day, I was reminded of an expression I often use, *"who would we be without each other, in our human family."*

Someone who appears to be a total stranger can be part of a greater family called our Soul family. We are all here to exchange light with each other through a touch, a smile, a glance, etc. all ways that remind us of who we really are on this earth, and why we have come here: to ground higher light on planet Earth, which raises the consciousness of humanity. We are doing that now.

I can only imagine the relief this man felt after having the courage to speak and share what was on his mind and in his heart. This illustrates the power of 'one' that can be shared in the most unlikely of circumstances. I encourage you when you are in public places to be open and at least say 'hello' to strangers, because YOU just might be exactly what they have been praying for.

The Pharmacy Dispenser

Amy works as a dispenser in a large city-center pharmacy that provides a methadone program for heroin users. Although it is against the rules of their recovery program many of the customers are still 'secretly' using. They come in to the pharmacy to get their prescribed methadone, which they then dilute and sell on the street to support their underground heroin addiction. They often steal products (to sell) from the pharmacy while they are waiting to get their prescription filled, as another way to get money to support their secret habit.

This is the only pharmacy in town that offers this methadone program, and many of the customers have already been blacklisted from pharmacies in other nearby towns for breaking the program rules, stealing, and other anti-social and/or abusive behavior. This pharmacy is the last chance for many of them to finally get clean and if they also get blacklisted from here, they have no hope of getting into another recovery program.

So how is Amy being a lightworker undercover in this situation? She is aware of the addicts' situation and it would be so easy for her to fall into judgment and fear. Instead she holds them in the light of love, and gives them great space for healing. She is firm with them, of course, yet she also recognizes the importance of giving them a chance. When she finds them stealing from the shop, she points out that this is the last pharmacy in town that will support them, and then she requests that they put back whatever they were about to take, and sit down while they wait.

This simple approach works because it builds trust and keeps the door open for them to recover. In addition to this, every time she clears out her closet at home she brings in old clothes and shoes which she keeps in the back of the store. If someone looks particularly in need she will just quietly give them whatever she thinks might fit that they could use. None of this is expected in her role as a pharmacy dispenser, and she certainly doesn't do it for praise or gratitude because that is more often not forthcoming from this particular customer base!

She is simply holding a light. Keeping a quiet but light presence, and holding a pure intention for them to get well. She holds them in her heart and in her prayers, and they can feel it. The regular addicts who return year in year out respect Amy and know that she is one of the few people who is helping them in a world where few people can or will. Who knows how many of them would not be here now if it were not for her shining her firm and steady light, in a dark place.

I know Amy and she is this way in every area of her life. It is an innate way of being for her, and that could make one wonder if people can learn to become that, which for her is innate. In my work with lightworkers (especially undercover lightworkers) I know that it can be learned. It can also become a way of life once you realize that you are a lightworker. Then what you do is what any lightworker would do in lightening up a situation. So I encourage you to look for signs in yourself and others that might be clues that you are here to bring more light to the planet. Acknowledge them, so that you can consciously begin turning up the dimmer switch for your light. We need more light on the planet for these dimming times.

A Letter To The Hotel Staff

What follows is a letter that I wrote to the hotel staff after a very difficult stay, about the ongoing lack of good service at a well known hotel. My young grandchildren were staying with me and they were treated by the staff very much unlike the guests that they were of this fine hotel. I sat with the situation and decided after three complaints to the front desk that I would write a letter to raise the consciousness of the staff, regarding the situation that I had experienced over four days. This is a very good example of how to lighten up a situation by shining light on the subject, as opposed to staying engaged at the level of 'the problem.'

The manager was very grateful that I took the time to do that and said he would be reading it at the next staff meeting. He was also going to send it to corporate headquarters for inclusion in the company magazine, to remind their employees of how important they are to the hotel guests. I want to point out again here that if I had just made an everyday complaint, with an emotional charge, as if I had been insulted, then that would have been me meeting them at the level of their unconscious vibration. What is elevating about this letter is not so much the actual words, but the energetic space I was in writing it: a space of compassion, higher love, and higher light, for the human beings involved. Their unkindness, insensitivity, and lack of compassion resulted not from them being 'bad people' but from whatever was going on in their home lives and work space that had them under so much pressure that they were 'leaking' their frustrations on the guests.

Dear family,
Yes, we are family. We are an important part of a greater family of human beings of all sizes, shapes, and colors. You and I, we, make up the kaleidoscope of humanity. Where would we be without each other? Especially when we are travelling and away from our local community of familiar friends and family.

This is where you come into the picture so very importantly. Every hello and every gesture, with a smile and a twinkle in your eye, says I matter to you. It says you care, and that you know we are connected in heart and soul, as a family of humanity.

Our collective life journey is meant to give us challenges that bring us together, so that we need each other's support in all the ways that we bring that to each other. I promise to contribute to you, all of you that I meet along the way, with a kind and generous spirit of co-operation in kindness, in the awareness that we are connected. Knowing that we are all here for each other, in service to the collective humanity in our own unique ways.

Working for the public can be challenging, just as depending on others when you are away from home can be as well. So, rather than giving you a list of the challenges I encountered at this hotel, I thought it best to remind you of how much you are needed and appreciated along the way, as we all journey together in this game of life that we are all playing together in so many different roles. I am grateful for you.

Thank you for being a part of my journey, no matter what role you played, I am better for it.

In appreciation, Anya Sophia Mann

I took me fifteen minutes to write that letter as the words from my heart just kept coming. The compassion I felt for the overworked staff was palpable. Yes, this *is* who we can be for each other, as we speak and give voice to the bigger picture rather than staying focused and agitated on the problem. For me, the best part is that I was the recipient of a gift: the gift of experiencing myself in the beautiful energy of higher light! That is the gift this experience gave me.

The School Teacher

It can take some time for us to develop our capacity for elevating situations by flowing light. At first, as we begin observing ourselves, we may find we spend more of our time acting out our shadow, than flowing our light. The key is to just keep going, and keep paying attention. We can begin by practicing small acts of kindness, whenever we can, and go from there.

One example of this is an elementary school teacher who works in a poor neighborhood where the parents often don't have jobs, and the kids don't have much. Because she works in one of the poorest school districts her salary isn't much either, yet she will do small things, like one week taking in some school paper supplies, another week it may be pens. Little by little these small acts of kindness build up, until being kind becomes a habit. Kindness will break the habit of acting out shadow behavior, and is a good way to start flowing your light.

"Be kind whenever possible. It is always possible"

- HH IV Dalai Lama

The children in this classroom are learning from the teacher, who is exemplifying small acts of kindness. They, in turn, started bringing in a small picked flower on the way to school or something from dollar store. The kindness soon spread to the other students. They would even put sticky notes - random sticky notes - on each other's desks, with happy faces and kind words. All it took was one teacher spreading her light to cause kindness to become contagious in the classroom.

Bellissima

Another way to shine your light is by accessing the power of the simple act of using terms of endearment. Can you imagine every time you walked into a room and your partner greeted you with bellissima? Bellissima is Italian for 'beautiful.' I remember one couple who had been married for over thirty-five years, yet every time they re-connected, at the beginning of the day or when he came home from work, he would greet his wife with 'bellissima.' Even though she heard it every day throughout their marriage, she would still light up every time. Greeting someone with 'hello handsome', 'hello love', 'hello sunshine', 'bellissima' or any term of endearment is a recognition that you see their light. It has the effect of lighting you both up even more.

Lightworker Qualities

The following poems reflect and draw forth some of the inner qualities of a conscious lightworker, one of which is the ability to listen with an open heart and an open mind:

Listen

*When I ask you to listen to me
and you start giving me advice,
you have not done what I asked.*

*When I ask you to listen to me
and you begin to tell me why
I shouldn't feel that way
you are trampling on my feelings.*

*When I ask you to listen to me
and you feel you have to do something
to solve my problem,
you have failed me,
strange as that may seem.*

*Listen! all I ask is that you listen
– not talk – or "do."
Just hear me.*

*When you do something for me
that I can do for myself,
you contribute to my fear and inadequacy.*

*But, when you accept as simple fact
that I do feel what I feel,
no matter how irrational,
then I can stop trying to convince you,
and get about the business of understanding
what's behind my feelings.*

*And, when it's clear to me
what's behind my feelings
the answers will become obvious,
and I won't need advice.*

So please, listen and just hear me.

*And, if you want to talk,
wait a minute for your turn,
and I'll listen to you.*

- author unknown

How I Define Myself

*I do not define myself by how many roadblocks
have appeared in my path.*

*I define myself by the courage
I've found to forge new roads.*

*I do not define myself
by how many disappointments I've faced.*

*I define myself by the forgiveness and the faith
I have found to begin again.*

I do not define myself by how long a relationship lasted.

*I define myself by how much I have loved,
and been willing to love again.*

*I do not define myself by how many times
I have been knocked down.*

*I define myself by how many times
I have struggled to my feet.*

*I am not my pain. I am not my past.
I am that which has emerged from the fire.*

- author unknown

You can see from the examples in this chapter that the world is full of undercover lightworkers quietly going about their everyday lives, grounding more light into the planet in a myriad of ways such as these poems. In other words, whether putting pen to paper, fingers to a keyboard, notes to a song, paint to a canvas, or voice to a poem, all are ways of grounding light through inspiration. I encourage you to act on your inspirations, especially now that you know they are ways of grounding light on the planet! The light *descends*, we ground it like grounding rods and then it *ascends*, expanding *us* with it.

Recharge and Regenerate

Because it can sometimes feel as though you are constantly 'on duty' it is also important that lightworkers find a place to recharge and regenerate. A favorite walk, or a meditation room (or both). This is your sacred space where you yourself receive support and are not getting drained. It is also important to pay attention to your feelings (as we mentioned in chapter eight) as you go through your day, to make sure you are always connected to your inner light, Source energy. If you find that you ARE feeling drained, those are the times that you have become distracted. Remember to go home to YOU, often.

Personal Responsibility

Taking personal responsibility for yourself is now more important than ever (as is getting your attention off other people) because you are not, and cannot be, responsible for others. You can support them on their journey but you cannot be responsible for them, because you cannot do their work for them. Just as you have to do your own work of clearing your own energy and flowing your light (as we mentioned in chapter eight), so do others. We are our own answer. This idea is worthy of sitting with until you can fully understand the reason for it and the importance of it.

Your Light Is Real And Is Felt As Love

Never doubt that the love and light you are flowing into the world is real and can be felt by those who are sensitive enough, other lightworkers. One time I was on a flight on my way to visit a friend when I became aware of a feeling of love as a warmth in my heart that was rising. When my friend met me at the airport I asked her if she had been flowing love to me while I was flying, and she confirmed that she had. I asked her if she knew what time that was, and she said, *"yes I looked at the clock."* Sure enough, it was at that exact time that I had felt it! This shows that when we send light it is received, even though the receiver may be unaware of it at the time! You are continuously exchanging frequencies and harmonizing with each other.

A great visual of how we flow and exchange energy with each other, is portrayed in the movie of James Redfield's book *"The Celestine Prophecy."* I highly recommend taking the time to visit this movie.

You Are Transferring Light

Being in the light of love when you are cooking, humming, singing etc. are other ways that you can simply flow light on an everyday level. What you hold in your heart moves out through your hands so it's also important when you touch people (even by cooking for them) to know that you are transferring light. Can food be sacred? Yes! What you're thinking, what you're saying, what you're feeling when you're working with it, affects it, either positively or negatively.

The sound of your voice and your thoughts are also vibrating to light. On one occasion I was in a meditation group and I looked up and could see thought forms coming out of people's heads, as geometric shapes in fluorescent colors! Everything is light and the more you allow yourself to align with the frequencies of light, the more you will become aware of the light that permeates everything we think of as our physical world. In fact, the more you attune to light, the 'lighter' and less physical our world appears. On another occasion I was walking along a river when the trees became streaks of light. I've never taken any drugs and the beauty in that for me is that I know this was a real altered-dimensional experience. For a brief time they didn't look like trees at all. These are some of the experiences you may find when you harmonize with light. When your perception shifts and you spend more time in clear space, the universe begins to reveal itself to you as it did that day when the trees lost their shape and it was pure energy flowing.

It was simply, as they say in the Tibetan Dzogchen tradition, reality appearing as *'the richness of dancing activities.'* This I believe is what I was seeing with my physical eyes that day. For me it was as if Life was giving me that experience to expand my conscious awareness that there is so much more going on than we can normally see with our physical eyes. Sharing this experience with you is a way that I am spreading my light. Every time lightworkers acknowledge and recognize one another's light we are *shining a light on lightworkers undercover.* ★

Chapter Eleven

The Light of The New Children

---

*"We must be the change
we wish to see in the world"*

- Mahatma Ghandi

The Light of The New Children

We have seen that as we live more fully in our light, to the point that it becomes who we are, our perception shifts and as a result our reality is different. As we become more aware of our light, and live every day, consciously flowing our light, we are contributing more light to the collective consciousness. This, in turn, contributes to the evolution of consciousness for the whole of humanity.

As we become more 'light' as a humanity, we will naturally develop higher capacities that result from our higher awareness and elevated perception. As we become more clear it is natural that our capacity for perception expands, just like when we stand on a mountain top we naturally have a wider vision of our surroundings: basically we can see more.

In our future as light beings, we will have capacities that are a natural result from our clear light and expanded perception, such as telepathy and clear knowing (clairvoyance). Future generations will be born with an even greater capacity for light than we have, and there seems to be evidence that the children being born now are already demonstrating this.

Have you noticed that the children around us are really bright lights in many ways? Meaning there is just something about them that appears to be more than what we were (or were allowed to be) at that age. Whether toddlers or teenagers there just seems to be something shining brighter in them as if they are plugged in to a knowing beyond this world.

Higher Light Frequency

That knowing seems to be connected to a higher consciousness or higher light frequency that is being grounded in our world. Higher Light as you can imagine will light a dark room or the darker side of humanity. In other words we can put light on the shadow aspects of ourselves, with more conscious awareness of how they show up in our lives. We mentioned in chapter eight how shadow aspects are always at the lower end of the spectrum of light and emotions. As the new children bring in a higher frequency, our shadow will become more visible. In other words anything that is not of the higher light, will come up into the light for healing. This is our opportunity to clearly see our shadow and consciously take steps to release our shadow aspects.

These new children have been given many names, for example the 'indigo' children[14] were thought to be some of the early wayshowers, clearing the path for those who would come later. Later, names such as 'crystal'[15], and 'rainbow' children were used. However these labels are now being dropped as these children are evolving and the references no longer fit the new iteration, not to mention these higher consciousness beings absolutely cannot and will not be boxed, controlled, or defined!

System Busters

Actually many of them are here as system-busters. System busters who cannot conform to the patriarchal systems inhibiting our expansion and evolution. These beings come

---

[14] "*The Indigo Evolution*" was a 2006 documentary directed by James Twyman and Kent Romney. See http://www.imdb.com/title/tt2853326/

[15] See "*The Children of Now: Crystalline Children, Indigo Children, Star Kids, Angels on Earth, and the Phenomenon of Transitional Children*" by Dr. Meg Blackburn Losey

fully expanded and we try to put them in a box. It will no
longer work because of who they are and what they're here to
do. This is just one of the ways that the old world that was
created in duality is dissolving, simply because it must as it
cannot survive in the unified field of oneness that we all will be
expressing and creating through.

Familial and societal conditioning such as *'Children
should be seen and not heard'* will not work on these new
children. They are here to bring us Unconditional Love and that
is precisely what we need to be in their presence. Many of them
have higher capacities such as high empathy and telepathy.
They often know what you are feeling before you know
yourself, so it is extremely important to be congruent in your
thoughts, feelings, words, and actions. They are sensitive and
will know if you are incongruent. Clear intention and attention
is now more important than ever as something to focus on
when interacting with these children.

Listening
Some of the new children are non-verbal, so listening becomes
a high priority. You need to listen to what is not being said.
Listening opens up your heart, and even increases your own

capacity for intuition and telepathic communication. Have you ever noticed that the word listen has the same letters as the word silent? This is your clue that the most effective listening happens when you can compassionately listen with an open heart and a quiet mind.

"A compassionate person is the most powerful healer, not only of their own disease or problems, but of those of others."

- Kyabje Lama Zopa Rinpoche

Before we speak to the consciousness of the new children let's take a look at consciousness itself. What is consciousness, or the light of consciousness? In my world consciousness is simply *clear space*. As we mentioned earlier, love is intelligent. Light is intelligent. There is no tiny atom in this whole universe, that does not contain light and love, so therefore, the whole universe is intelligent, alive and awake. This is consciousness. The whole universe is conscious in that it is aware. So consciousness really is, in it's highest sense, the awareness that IS the Universe and all within it, including us.

Intelligent light.

Light carries messages. Light in and of itself is a messenger. Like the notes on a scale that becomes a symphony we ourselves are carriers of a unique note in the symphony of light that is harmonizing humanity. We can best understand this, when we think of fiber-optic cable that has the capacity to transmit huge volumes of information – using light. When we see cable TV, we forget that the images that we are seeing have travelled along that cable in the form of light. When we use our high speed internet, we forget that we are transmitting information literally at the speed of light, because our internet cable is actually using light to transmit the information. Ordinary, everyday light, is intelligent and carries messages.

The New Consciousness

Through carrying a higher light, the new children are able to carry the new consciousness. What are some of the qualities of the new consciousness? The new children are highly empathic and telepathic. Telepathic meaning the ability to sense and feel others over distance. I am reminded of a telepathic impression that I received in the dream state, before my granddaughter was born. I did not know the sex of the baby and a month before she was born I saw in my minds' eye an infant sleeping. I knew then that it was a girl and also I heard in my head, "she will come in on the song of a singing bird, and you can see the reflection of the moon in her liquid ebony eyes." That is exactly what unfolded! I was sitting reading when I became

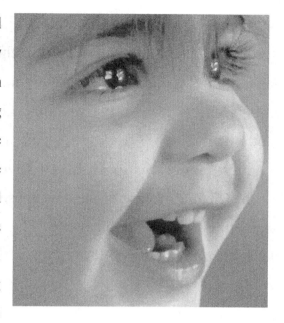

distracted by the length of time a beautiful songbird was singing. I looked to my left out the window as a bird took flight and landed in the tree directly outside the windows on the right. The song of this bird continued, getting louder and longer, and in came a text announcing the birth of a baby girl! Not only did she arrive on the song of a singing bird, but also you really can see the moon in her liquid ebony eyes!

The new children also embody higher mind, higher heart, and higher love. They come from oneness, so they don't know separation. They don't know duality. The world they are here to create will not be a dualistic world, yet the world they are born into is of duality. The higher light that they carry is needed to put light on the dualistic thinking that has created separation. Separation being: me-you, this-that, black-white, right-wrong, 'My way or the high way' power-over (authoritarianism), 'I know; you don't', teacher-student, superior-inferior, rich-poor, have's have-not's, and so forth and so on. The higher light of the new consciousness does not know separation, duality, or hierarchy. The thought 'I am (we are) better-than-you' does not even exist in their world.

The Autistic Spectrum

Some of the new children are being diagnosed on the autistic spectrum. Speech language pathologist and multidimensional communication expert Suzy Miller in her book *"Awesomism: A New Way To Understand The Diagnosis of Autism,"* noticed that the energy of children on the autistic spectrum was somehow 'different.' In her work Suzy suggests that a possible reason that some of them don't speak, or can't walk, may be because they are not integrating into the lower three chakras and are energetically only staying in the higher chakras, which means that they are connected to a higher consciousness. In other words they carry and emanate higher light through their consciousness on this planet, and that higher light is awakening all of us to our higher light. So these children are highly telepathic, empathic, and clairvoyant, simply because they are in tune with their higher light.

The new children are also very heart connected. It's heart centered connection that will prevail in our future world. Telepathic communication will be common. Fewer words will be used because there'll be a direct connection to the collective consciousness of humanity, through the messages carried on light.

An Ancient Lineage of Light

Earlier we talked about some of the scientific research that is demonstrating now that we are beings of light[16]. So we can see how the new children are the latest iteration in an ancient lineage of light beings. Some of us came in decades earlier, to pave the way, setting a foundation to make it easier for those who would come later, so that a higher elevation of consciousness could begin to be grounded on the planet.

When I say the lineage of light I'm referring to the holders

---

[16] See the work of Dr Fritz Albert Popp mentioned in chapter one.

of light, keepers of the light, lightworkers, Masters of light and Ambassadors of light: beings whose physicality in all of it's wonder: brain, organs, skeletal structure, nervous system, is all wired and being attuned *to be able to process and integrate the refined Divine Light* that they carry. We know about the early avatars such as Christ and Buddha, but there are also many beings who we never hear about who carry a higher light yet live an ordinary everyday lifestyle. Are they better than anyone else? No they are simply high frequency beings, here to balance and harmonize lower frequencies to create a beautiful symphony, where every player has a role. No one more important than the other, in the game of life where we are all harmonizing for a whole new humanity to create a whole new world. One in which the highest expression of higher light and love in oneness will be the dominant vibration.

Social and Familial Conditioning

One of the greatest challenges for the new children comes from the conditioning that we're unconsciously laying on them. We're trying to make them be like us, and they're not. They can't be. They are here to break the lineage of karmic, societal, and familial conditioning that all of us have molded into, and bring in a new unconditioned humanity. The biggest of that conditioning happens the first day of school when the free-spirited child has to conform to the academic culture which permeates an undercurrent of 'this is the way we do things around here' that each child absorbs like a sponge. This cultural conditioning sounds like, *"my mother said...,"* *"our church does it this way...,"* and *"my education taught me..."* etc.

Source Light Never Changes

That is how the 'shadows' begin to overlay the light that they carry, like clouds that appear to block out the light of the sun. We know the clouds aren't really dimming the sun's light, but they appear to. So the shadows appear to weaken our connection to the Source of that Divine Light. The Source light never changes, it's the overlay on it, like when you put sunglasses on you are filtering the light, and the messages from that light. The light hasn't changed it just appears to. If you look into the eyes of a child and say *"you are light, and light you shall remain"* they will not argue that, because every cell in their body raises its vibration because it's just been called up into the light that's emanating throughout the being. This is what I would whisper into the ears of my children as they were sleeping!

*"These kids are tuned into a certain frequency all the time ...
these new children are not plugged into their parents lineage.
That is why they are here to bring in a new humanity."*

- Suzy Miller, Author of "Awesomism"

I was fortunate to be able to work with Suzy Miller, and to participate in her awesomism practitioner process for three and a half years, where I had the opportunity to connect with the consciousness of many children, and the collective consciousness of people on the autistic spectrum ranging from non-verbal to savant. This is where I realized that I too am on that spectrum. I mean that from the place of having extraordinarily heightened abilities in the realm of everything intuitive.

Why You Don't Fit In - You're Wired Differently

Some of us will come to find out that we are just wired differently and, as a result, we may be treated like we don't fit in. What might really be going on is that we are born with a skill set that can raise the frequency of every human being as a collective, through the individual. Many of us emanate an energy that restores balance to any situation.

I think of Shirley MacLaine's book *"Out On A Limb"* where, after a very long, hard, spiritual journey, she proclaimed the realization from deep within her that God is not out there, that we are a part of God. As she claimed the words 'I am God' everything in her being lit up, in that knowing. I am also reminded of Gregg Braden's book *"The Divine Matrix"* where he demonstrates how the 'signature cell' of God is within every human being! That deepens my understanding of the Indian greeting 'Namaste', often loosely translated as *'God in me recognizes God in you.'*

There Is No Separation

From the perspective of unity consciousness there is no separation between us and God. The new children are connected to their higher light, through this oneness. It's like watching an autistic child with a glow light, who is lost in it, mesmerized by the light. What if that mesmerizing was a remembering of the light from where we came? When they look up at a chandelier, and they're lost in it for three hours, what if that's them connecting with higher consciousness? It is certainly possible, through the information that is carried within light, that the rainbow light of the chandelier gets their attention and then they begin resonating to the frequency of oneness and unity. This could even be called 'remembering home.'

I can relate to this feeling, which I often feel in a meditative state when my mind is clear and my body is still. In that place a vibrant expansion of my being is felt and in that, the sensed parameters of my body dissolve. A merging and a oneness is experienced in the depth of the expansion, as if connected to all things with no thought about them. Often in that state wisdom arises from higher mind as a knowing that's beyond anything learned. I can only imagine how flowing that energy into worldly situations, by simply sitting in that state, will positively influence outcomes.

Innate Wisdom

The new children also carry innate wisdom that comes from the clear intelligent light of unity consciousness. They just 'know' things that are not mental constructs. In the Tibetan tradition this is known as 'clear light knowing.' As they become conditioned by the society around them they start to lose some of their clarity and wisdom. This happens around aged five but up until then they often have clear memory of wisdom from previous lifetimes. For example one day my grandson leapt up in the air and landed in a meditation posture saying, *"Nana will you teach me this?"* I asked, *"how do you know this?"* and he said, *"I saw a picture of it in school."*

He was referring to the lotus position often used in yoga and meditation. His body posture was perfect right down to the fact that he was doing hand mudras, even though he didn't consciously 'know' what they were, but nobody had taught him! There was even a peaceful contemplative look on his face. So how did he know? These children 'just know.'

These children carry a field of grace and it's in the field of grace that all the transformation and transcendence is happening. In that environment magic beyond comprehension can happen!

---

*"And when you have gone beyond being human you will,
without any doubt, become an angel; you will be done with
earth, and heaven will be your home. Go beyond even that
angelic condition. Dive again into God's boundless ocean. So
your drop of water at last transforms into the sea."*

\- Rumi

It is possible to connect with these beings telepathically.
What follows is some information that was brought through, as
a result of connecting with the consciousness of these children
for over three years. You can see that it's very musical,
melodical, poetic. This particular example is of a telepathic
connection with a young teenager, at the higher end of the
autistic spectrum. One beautiful sunny day I was out walking
alone, and in my mind I asked William, *"what do you want me
to know about the world you come from? and is there a
message for us in this earthly dimension?"*

The reply came in as one block of information, and felt
like I was listening to a poem from Rumi that had been put to
music. It was very melodic in it's resonance, and simple in it's
delivery, making my felt understanding of the information

palpable and almost beyond words in it's clarity and wisdom[17].

> **Higher Light To You**
>
> *For and from the love of you*
> *- we come*
>
> *You are our grounding force*
> *- transmission towers*
>
> *As above so below*
> *- grounded light*
>
> *We meet in the now of you*
> *- presence*
>
> *When you meet Higher Light*
> *- it becomes you*
>
> *Density dissolves in surrender*
> *- awareness lightens*
>
> *Clear you for us as you*
> *- one us*
>
> *You asked we heard*
> *- listen silent*
>
> *New Children New You*
> *- New World*
>
> *You are us*
> *- bridge*
>
> *Love leads*
> *- follow love*
>
> *- from William (via Anya)*

---

[17] For me, words are vibrations and frequencies that I simply sense and feel first, then the words (of that vibration and frequency) follow. Often it feels from these children on the spectrum that a whole new language is needed, and then again as I say it, perhaps is not needed! I know you get the point!

Is something in you feeling called to elevate your life to a higher level and become everything you are capable of being in this life? The collective consciousness of the new children, no matter their age, is pulsing a light for you to recognize, and awaken in you the remembrance of who you really are – a being of light. Here to align, attune, and allow the light of the Divine to move through you in a myriad of forms of which compassionate action, self love, and self empowerment, are needed to ignite and support a more empowered humanity. In that empowerment you are your own authority and the chances of something being imposed on you from outside of you is very unlikely.

Illumined Conversations

In future we will live in a world that is much more unified in the oneness of humankind. This enlightened perspective reflects an illuminating conversation that is already happening on a cellular level, which is becoming an inspired emerging vocalization in our collective consciousness. Illumined conversations are beginning to bridge the gaps created by disconnection and separation, which are mending and healing in the awakening of the new energy of higher light, brightening the hearts and minds of all of us as we emerge into a new world that we all are co-creating.

A mystery of light is melting a frozen disconnected aspect of humanity that shows up in acts of great unconscious cruelty. The light of the Divine is showing up more and more, to illuminate this aspect, as each individual says 'no' to anything less than the truth of the connected unified oneness that we are. Waves of light are rippling through the ocean of human consciousness, elevating and illuminating the heart, soul, and consciousness of humanity and the planet, through the new children. The universal effect is immeasurable.

We are here as beings of light to create a unified reality. The children are here to support that, as are you as a conscious co-creator playing your role in the creation of a new way of being in a new world that you and I came for. As lightworkers we will remember and recognize ourselves in *the light of the new children*. ★

Chapter Twelve

Can YOU Hear The Call?

---

*"Our separation from each other
is an optical illusion of consciousness"*

\- Albert Einstein

Can YOU Hear The Call?

My hope for you (and wish for me), is that the words on the pages of this book act like pulsing beacons of light, calling you up and calling you forward, to more fully step into the brilliance YOU bring, as a unique Being of Light. Deep inside we all know that we are so much more than this world is telling us we are.

Our conditioning, commercials and schooling, no longer meet us where we are in our evolution of consciousness. There is a quiet calling that is really getting louder and louder amongst people, for change to happen. YOU are a big part of that change.

"No problem can be solved from the same level of consciousness that created it."
- Albert Einstein

You carry a consciousness that perceives things differently and you are meant to share your perception, your unique view, in as many ways and expressions as you can. We need all of us to shine what we value most. Shine it out into a world waiting for the creations only you can offer through your thoughts, words, deeds and conscious, compassionate, actions and creations. More and more people are able to recognize your light now, as a way of being reminded that they too are beings of light. We no longer need to work undercover, hiding our light to fit in.

See The Light In Others

Seeing the light around and within everyone we encounter is becoming more and more important as a way forward, in an otherwise shadowed world of people acting out from separation. They are screaming to us that they are in pain, and are suffering in the illusion of being disconnected from all of us, which in their world may show up as loss of physical home, job, car, family, divorce, etc. and it goes on and on and on to the point where one no longer need to wonder, how did we get like this? How did it get so bad? Wonder no more. It is in plain light now. Violent acts come from people who feel lost, alone, abandoned, separate, like misfits and black sheep in the family of humanity. Does reading that cause the warmth of a flame to glow in your heart that wants to brighten and transmit the energy of love and light to your brothers and sisters in our family who are hurting?

Generate A Field of Grace

Throughout the book we have seen how ordinary people can generate a powerful *field of grace* through heart-centered acts of compassion in their everyday lives and work. People like you. Some recognize themselves as lightworkers and some don't. My heartfelt wish is for you to now take up the call, and recognize yourself as a lightworker. This book calls you up to be more aware of the light you carry, and the positive impact your light has on others.

Key Quotes

The following table is a brief summary of each chapter in the form of key quotes that you can use as a prompt to share in your world and remind you of who you really are.

Key Quotes from Each Chapter

Chapter One
You, as a unique ray of light in the body of humanity, are aware and know
in the peace of your heart and Soul that the light of love will change the world.

Chapter Two
You know you're a lightworker when you recognise yourself as a being of light,
and a lightworker knows a lightworker.

Chapter Three
With every word, deed, and action, a lightworker consciously knows they matter
to everything coming into their awareness and beyond.

Chapter Four
You carry a very unique ray, a unique shade, a unique shape, of light
that is making an essential contribution to the kaleidoscope of humanity.

Chapter Five
Like a child at play be the brightest light in the room, even if you're sitting
in the corner, and remember there are degrees of that brightness.

Chapter Six
We can dance in our own light bringing beautiful music to our world
and harmonising the symphony of humanity through light.

Chapter Seven
The difference that you make in bringing more light to this planet, is beyond measure.

Chapter Eight
Feeling the power of your light source is all about paying attention
to what you are feeling. Your feelings are your guidance system.

Chapter Nine
What's true for you IS the truth in that moment,
and your truth is ever-evolving.

Chapter Ten
An undercover lightworker will often never see the result of their 'infusion of light',
which points to the fact that they are not motivated by recognition.

Chapter Eleven
The collective consciousness of the new children is pulsing light
to awaken in you the remembrance of who you really are.

Chapter Twelve
More and more people are able to recognise your light now
as a way of being reminded that they too are a Being of Light.
We no longer need to work undercover, hiding our light to fit in.

Six Questions

The following six questions are for you to simply ponder from the place in your heart that already knows the answer. In doing so, you may come to recognize your light more deeply.

Who – did I come here to be?

What – am I here to do and bring in service to humanity?

Where – in my home, work or community, can I shine my unique light and speak more with the language of light that illuminates shadows?

When – will I decide, now is the time to fully show up as a lightworker in the world?

Why – am I the one to shine the light?
The answer is clearly, who are you not to be?
This is why you came.

How – can I be of more service to my fellow brothers and sisters in humankind, to support their awakening to the fact that we are beings of light?

Your Journey of Light

This life is a journey. On this journey it is not so much that we are going anywhere it's more about what are we learning, because that is what is evolving us. There is no destination, yet we must still set off on our own personal journey to discover that truth for ourselves. Joseph Campbell in his book *"The Hero With A Thousand Faces"* describes three stages that we all experience on our path:

1.   **Separation**
2.   **Initiation**
3.   **Return**

Through this journey we will all come to the place where we see the light in ourselves and each other. We can see these three paths in every hero's journey through popular movies such as Star Wars, where the hero Luke Skywalker is initially separated from his family, then initiated into the ways of the Jedi, and then finally returns with his new-found knowledge to save the day. Does he return to his family? No, his family are gone. After his long and arduous journey he finally returns home to himself. He recognizes his own light.

"We must be willing to let go of the life we planned so as to have the life that is waiting for us."

– Joseph Campbell, mythologist, writer and lecturer.

Once you fully embrace your power and role as a lightworker then you become an *ambassador of light*. Who is an ambassador of light? An ambassador of light is an empowered human being aware that the light of love will change the world. Imagine that, imagine walking around knowing yourself to be, claiming yourself to be, and stepping up and stepping into, *"I am an ambassador of light."* It's like a representative, let's say an ambassador of peace, an ambassador of peace is a representative of that peace within the being and within the world. An ambassador shows up when the light is calling them forward to go into areas, whether it's a conversation or a dark street or wherever the shadows are, the light will show up in just being, just by shining that light.

Lightworkers know that just by bringing a world event into their consciousness, into their hearts, they can help to shift the energy from fear to love. I can't emphasize enough how important it is that you *recognize your own light.* You *are* on a journey. Sometimes your journey will take great courage. Often you will not be seen by others around you. Often you will be misunderstood. Like Luke Skywalker, or the hero in Mary Oliver's famous poem *"The Journey."* Yet journey on you must. Why? *Because it is who you are.* You are on your own journey home to YOU. To discover your own light.

"there was a new voice,
which you slowly
recognized as your own,
that kept you company
as you strode deeper and deeper
into the world"

- Mary Oliver
from *"The Journey"* in *"Dream Work"*

The first time I read this poem[18] tears of soulful recognition streamed down my face. I felt seen and heard more deeply than ever. May you too recognize yourself and your journey in this lightworkers' brilliant work of poetic art.

---

[18] Read "The Journey" by Mary Oliver at
http://static.oprah.com/images/201104/omag/the-journey.pdf

My prayer for all of us is that we each light up our world like the north star, and twinkle like fairy dust, as we dance the light of our being in cohesive harmony, co-creating the magic of higher love in the light of our divinity. We are what we have been waiting for.

Can YOU hear the call?

Lightworker Undercover – Your Time is NOW!

About The Author

Anya Sophia Mann is a transformational author, speaker, seminar-leader and visionary intuitive consultant. She believes in living on purpose and shining your highest light in the world.

Her joy in life is supporting people in shifting perspectives so that they come to know themselves fully, as spiritual beings. She presents radio shows, workshops and tele-gatherings, offers coaching, consulting and mentoring, writes books, blogs and poetry to support people in being heart-centered enlightened leaders in their own lives and businesses, by recognizing their light and living it.

Family, friends, nature, world-travel, rich conversations, beautiful music and meaningful connections fill her days with love.

Anya creates power programs, webinars and retreat workshops on timely topics like REAL Personal Power for personal and professional success in life, business, and beyond.

"It is my heartfelt intention that you will see yourself in the light of this book. If that is so I would love to hear from you, and invite you to connect with other Souls like you on our Facebook page"

- Anya

https://www.facebook.com/GlobalLightworkers/

Web: http://AnyaSophiaMann.com

eMail: Anya@AnyaSophiaMann.com

Twitter: @AnyaSophiaMann @GlobalLightwork

Facebook: http://www.facebook.com/AnyaSophiaMann

https://www.facebook.com/GlobalLightworkers/

Other Titles by This Author:

In The Light of A New Day:
Enlightenment For Everyday Living

Gems For YOU:
Daily Gems of Wisdom (Book 1)

Anya Sophia Mann is also a contributing author to the following titles:

The View:
Heart over Mind, Mind over Matter

Unwavering Strength:
Stories To Inspire You Through Challenging Times

Unwavering Strength:
Volume 2, Stories To Warm Your Heart and Soul

Made in the USA
Coppell, TX
10 December 2019

12715030R10125